In the Bag!

LABRADOR TRAINING FROM PUPPY TO GUNDOG

In the Bag!

LABRADOR TRAINING FROM PUPPY TO GUNDOG

MARGARET ALLEN

THE CROWOOD PRESS

First published in 2013 by
The Crowood Press Ltd
Ramsbury, Marlborough
Wiltshire SN8 2HR

www.crowood.com

British Library Cataloguing-in-Publication Data
A catalogue record for this book is available from the British Library.

ISBN 978 1 84797 481 5

Acknowledgements
I am sincerely indebted to the many people I have met over the years
who have taught me so much about dogs and how they think. I would
especially like to thank the following people: John Brentnall, MRCVS,
and Terence Girling, MRCVS, for vetting the veterinary bits of this book;
Tony Jackson and Sue Orr for their encouragement and proof reading;
Paul Quagliana, Hubert Watlington and Sophie Ross Gordon for photo-
graphs; Andy Hodder and his crew for their patience and help with
photocopying; and Jenny Barber, Shirley Wood, Cheryl Wheeler and
Ross Morland, who have helped in so many ways to enable me to get
on with writing this book. Above all, I am so very grateful to my family,
friends and the many Labradors who were the inspiration for me to start
and complete this book.

Typeset by Jean Cussons Typesetting, Diss Norfolk

Printed and bound in India by Replika Press Pvt Ltd

CONTENTS

FOREWORD

The art of preparing a gundog for successful work in the field is a skill that requires in the trainer a subtle understanding of animal psychology, combined with the practical application of carefully considered training methods. So often for the amateur or the first-time owner of a young dog hopefully being trained for the shooting field, problems arise due in part to a failure to understand the mentality of the animal or, as is so often the case, an understandable but flawed desire to impose lessons well in advance of the dog's still juvenile comprehension.

Margaret Allen, whom I have known for many years, is one of that select group of gundog trainers who, having studied the behaviour and mental processes of gundogs, has applied training methods that are based on an understanding of just what it is that makes a dog tick. In the far distant past dogs, whatever their breed or purpose, were trained by 'breaking', involving methods that were harsh and today would be considered cruel. However, in the post-war era a new method of training was developed by the late Peter Moxon, a pioneer in the field of dog psychology and understanding, and this has been developed and adopted by subsequent successful trainers.

Many of Margaret's dogs have won in field trials, working tests and in the show ring, and she and her team of Labradors are greatly in demand for picking-up at local shoots each season. Furthermore, as well as running a successful kennel business, she organizes popular training classes, both for beginners and for more experienced owners.

In this, her first book, Margaret has distilled the knowledge gained over the years, and while she accepts that there are many different ways to teach a dog, there are certain basics that are common to all, and as a result she has developed a method which certainly works for her and the dogs she has had the pleasure of training over the years.

Margaret has greatly helped me train my own Labradors, and I cannot emphasize too highly her skills and her patience, not only with her canine charges but also with their owners! This book is, I sincerely believe, essential reading, not only for the beginner setting out to train his or her first retriever, but also for the more experienced owner.

Tony Jackson
Tatworth
Somerset 2012

PREFACE

My purpose in writing this book is to give would-be dog trainers an understanding of dog psychology as I perceive it, and to see how it can be used to train and handle your Labrador successfully. I believe that by using the methods described here, you will achieve the best possible result with your dog. You will be, and, I hope, be seen to be, humane. Your dog will respect you and be happy in all his dealings with you. He will understand you and he will give of his best.

This is not a book of political correctness. Dogs have not heard of political correctness. Dogs do not understand political correctness. They cannot understand it and they never will. What they do understand are the rules of the wild pack. Thousands of years and generations of domestication have not changed this. They are happy with their way of life and their perceptions of what is right and wrong. They feel secure and content when the pack guidelines are in place. We are intelligent and adaptable enough to understand this. It is up to us to work out how their mind works. Only when we see things the way they do can we make the connection that leads to a partnership with our dog.

This is not a book for remedial cases. Instances where dogs have got off to a bad start through the harshness, over-indulgence or negligence of their owner is not really within the scope of this treatise. However, I would expect that if my methods are used on a promising dog, albeit a psychologically damaged one, varying degrees of success may be gained.

I believe that breeding plays a great part in the making of a good dog. It will influence many aspects of the animal, including temperament, intelligence, trainability, sagacity, physical soundness, looks and courage. For this reason I have given my opinions on choosing your dog.

I also believe that you are what you eat, and so I have included ideas about feeding dogs that I have found to work well. Along with feeding comes management, so there is a bit about housing, exercise and veterinary matters.

I once asked a man who had done over 80,000 hours of sailing by himself, what he thought was the most important thing in life. 'Timing,' he said.

Astonished, I said, 'But what about love?'

'Timing takes care of love,' he replied. 'Timing takes care of everything.'

How very true I have found this to be, and never more so than in dog training. If you have the timing right, you will make good progress. If you persistently get it wrong, you will make only slow progress, or none at all. Most people are not quick enough to anticipate what their dog is going to do next, but with concentration, effort and practice, this can be improved.

Perfection does not exist in this world, and we cannot all act or react in exactly the right way or at exactly the right moment every time. This does not mean that we shouldn't aim for a star – we might hit a tall tree!

INTRODUCTION

I was brought up in Bermuda: my father was eighth generation Bermudian, my mother fourth generation. When I was growing up we always had a dog, but I thought that the only things a dog could learn were the whistle that brought him in for supper and the word 'Gertcha!' meaning 'Get out of it!'

In late 1955, when I was eleven, an American lady came to Bermuda and gave lectures on dog training and held a few classes. Immediately I was hooked. I put our ten-year-old cocker spaniel, Rusty, through the exercises day after day. Shortly after that, we emigrated from Bermuda to Edmonton in Western Canada, where my father flew as a bush pilot. Rusty stayed in Bermuda with my grandparents. In Edmonton there was a dog training club. I was over the moon. We soon acquired a dog from the Society for the Prevention of Cruelty to Animals kennels, a male Husky cross Collie named Skipper. He was a wonderful dog and desperate to learn. He won many competitions for me. When we returned to Bermuda in 1959, he came with us and adjusted well to the new life and climate. In those days dogs were allowed to wander and were seldom neutered. Forty-odd years later you could still see Skipper types around the island!

My mother's sister was one of the first people to bring Labradors into Bermuda. That was in the early 1960s. As soon as I laid eyes on them, I thought, 'That's for me!' A few years later, when I was married and living in England, my husband gave me a yellow Labrador bitch that we named Christy. I gave her basic training at the local obedience club, and my husband took her rough shooting where she did the job of both spaniel and retriever.

When we decided to breed from her, we were lucky enough to be put in touch with Mrs Audrey Radclyffe, who had the Zelstone Labradors. We used the dog she recommended, and in due course a litter of six delightful pups was born. Mrs Radclyffe said that if I kept a puppy I should bring it to her retriever training classes. But Christy was unregistered, and by now I had realized that I should acquire a registered puppy; so we found good homes for all the pups, and with Mrs Radclyffe's guidance I bought a yellow bitch named Crystal Clare whom we called Tally. She was by Zelstone Brandysnap and out of a bitch named Sally Sel.

We attended the classes and both learnt a great deal. Tally was a clever, willing dog and came first in nearly every competition in which she ran. She won her first field trial, which was also my first. Since then I have had many Labradors, golden retrievers, springer spaniels and cockers, but I'm sure that the Labrador will always be my favourite. Many of my dogs have won in working tests, field trials and in the show ring, and I have had a lot of fun and pleasure with them.

In 1984 I was working as a secretary for a very demanding man. One day I woke up and said to myself, 'I'm quitting this job and never working for anyone else again.' Of course, one is nearly always working for someone else, even if it's just for the taxman! I then had to decide what I could do well enough to earn a living. Having trained my own dogs and helped other people with theirs, I thought I would set up a training kennel. If it didn't work out, it could be turned into a cattery.

It worked out. I have learned a great deal over the years and am still learning. There are hundreds of different types of dog and hundreds of different ways to teach each one of them, but there are certain basics to the method I have developed, and this book is about them.

CHAPTER 1

LOOK BEFORE YOU LEAP

Perhaps you picked up this book because you are thinking about acquiring a working Labrador Retriever. Possibly you already have a Labrador, but in case you haven't, or are looking for another one, you may find the following helpful.

Turning your hobby into your work is a glad and sorry thing, but that is what I did. My life has revolved around dogs for many years, and when anyone asks me what I do for a living, I say, 'Anything that's legal to turn a buck with gundogs!' But sometimes I feel like David Niven, who said something along the lines of: 'A writer is someone who wanders about the house in his dressing gown, drinking endless cups of coffee and lost for words.' There are times when I would rather do almost anything other than train a dog.

Animals are seven days a week, and dogs are no exception. They need frequent, regular attention, which means providing food, water, shelter, exercise, training and control. Knowledge becomes necessary so that you can spot when your dog needs medical attention, and then you may need to devote many hours to his care and rehabilitation. Having adequate time to see to all these things is essential, so before you begin, examine your situation and decide honestly whether you have the time to give a dog its fair share of attention.

WHAT IS A LABRADOR RETRIEVER?

Labradors first appeared in Great Britain in the early part of the nineteenth century, brought in from Newfoundland and Labrador, Canada, although probably their earliest forebears originated in Europe. It is interesting to note that the Portuguese cattle dog and the Labrador look remarkably similar to one another.

The Kennel Club breed standard, although open to the interpretation of the reader, gives a good guideline to the appearance and nature of the correct Retriever (Labrador), as they like to call him. However, the breed today is numerically very strong, and thousands of breeders, imagining their ideal Labrador, have all made their contribution. Thus the Labrador Retriever these days comes in a variety of shapes and sizes, although it is extraordinary to note that most Labrador puppies of four and five weeks of age look very much alike, even though they may be from parents of widely differing types.

In appearance my ideal Labrador is a strong, sound, active dog of medium size, with no exaggeration in any point. From the front his limbs should appear straight with good bone, and when viewed from the side, the legs should have good angulation. He should appear to move with an economy of action, smoothly and freely in all paces. He should have a thick, water-resistant coat and a tail like an otter. This tail should wag almost constantly, often thumping his flanks on either side. The permitted colours are black, yellow (which may range from cream to fox-red) and liver. Except for a small spot on the chest, white markings are not allowed. His ears should not be big or hound-like, and his feet should be neatly rounded. He should have a kind, enthusiastic expression and a dark brown eye, and he should look at you honestly as though hoping to discover just what it is that you want him to do. An added bonus is for him to have good pigment – a friend of mine calls this 'lots of mascara'.

His stamina and athleticism should be outstanding, and his sense of smell exceptionally well developed. Good temperament is paramount: he should be confident, friendly and willing to please. I would want him to be intelligent; not wily, but clever and cooperative.

Crystal Clare – 'Tally' – my first registered Labrador and my ideal as regards conformation.

I would want him to be brave, to try hard but not be thoughtless or impetuous. He should not be a good guard dog or be aggressive in any way. A Labrador should have an extremely strong will to retrieve. Throughout his life, a true Labrador is happiest when he has something in his mouth. Of course, food is his favourite thing, but he just loves to carry things about.

WHY DO WE NEED A RETRIEVER?

When shooting game – and this is meant to include duck, pheasant, grouse, rabbit, hare and similar quarry – it is important to recover what is shot. Not only is it important from a wish not to waste good food, but also to get wounded game to hand as quickly as possible for humane dispatch. This is especially important these days when field sports are under keen scrutiny from those who seek to legislate against them.

Game often falls out of sight and in inaccessible places. A Labrador with courage and a good nose, and which is capable of being directed to the area where you believe the game lies, will usually find it for you.

WHAT DO WE REQUIRE OF OUR LABRADOR?

When a client brings me a dog to train, he often says, 'I don't want a Field Trial Champion, just a useful, obedient shooting dog.'

I then ask if he wants the dog to be steady, walk to heel, come when he is called, take whistle and hand signals, enter water and cover, and retrieve to hand. 'Oh yes,' comes the reply.

'Well, that is just what a Field Trial Champion has to do,' say I.

A retriever is required to walk to heel off lead, to

ABOVE: Labrador puppies love to carry things about.

RIGHT: Why we need a retriever – Labrador bringing a wounded partridge to hand, head up, eye bright.

sit quietly and calmly during drives, or whenever and wherever instructed. He may have to sit patiently for long periods of time. He should be seen but not heard. He should stop on the whistle and take hand signals at a distance. He should hunt where told, confidently and perseveringly. He must retrieve tenderly and to hand with the minimum of delay. It is desirable that he should be happy in water and be a strong swimmer. He should enter thick cover willingly, and be agile and able enough to jump reasonable obstacles.

In addition to all this, there are certain social graces that any gundog should possess. He should be quiet and well behaved in the car, house and kennel, and not go through doorways or get into or out of the car until bidden. He should be agreeable with people and other dogs, and affable about sharing his vehicle with others. He should not take an unhealthy interest in stock or cats.

SETTING ABOUT IT

When Should You Buy?

If possible, it is probably best to acquire your dog early in the year but after the shooting season is over. You will then have all the better weather and more daylight hours to get to know each other and to progress with the training, or in the case of the trained dog, to bond with him and get ready for the coming season.

If you decide on a puppy, it is so much easier to house-train him in the good weather than it is in the winter months. Often the door to the outside can be left open, and even if the puppy doesn't realize he should go out to do his 'business', you can hurry him out when you see the signs.

In the spring and summer you have more daylight in which to go out for training and interesting excursions where he will learn about the country where you live, fences and hedges and how to negotiate them, as well as different types of cover. He can also learn to enjoy water at a time when it is not dangerously turbulent. The water will also be a relatively pleasant temperature, although most dogs seem not to care when it is cold, and it amazes me to see adult dogs leap into icy water to retrieve in the winter.

Which Line?

Make sure that the Labrador you are contemplating acquiring has a pedigree and is registered with The

Labradors typical of the standard – father (black) with sons from different dams.

Kennel Club. If the dog turns out to be special you will probably want to breed from it. If you don't have its pedigree you can't be sure that the dog you plan to mate it to is not too closely related. In addition you may have difficulty in selling the puppies if there is no pedigree. If a dog is not registered, its progeny will not be registerable, which may also be a stumbling block when selling. Furthermore, many competitive events are open only to registered dogs.

Another point about pedigrees is that you can see how much show blood, if any, there is. Some people like their dogs to have a splash of show blood, whilst to others it is anathema.

The Labrador breed standard was drawn up by people who knew what was required of a good shooting dog. Gundogs must sometimes work for long hours in harsh weather conditions, cold water and dense cover. Certain breed points reflect this. The breed standard requires the dog to have a dense double coat that turns off water and prevents it from penetrating to the skin. It also requires that the dog has substance and strength so that he can withstand long periods waiting in the cold, and then have the stamina for prolonged hunting. The breed points were drawn up for good reasons. I like a dog to be within the standard in appearance as far as is possible, as well as having a talent for work, and the right temperament.

Considering that you may be looking at your dog for the next twelve or fourteen years, his appearance should please you. If it does not, you may come to love him 'warts and all', but there is also a chance that your dislike of his appearance will prejudice you against his character, an attitude you may never overcome.

If, in your prospective dog's immediate pedigree, you see the name of a dog that you know to have a bad fault – say, hard mouth, noisiness, nervousness or aggression – you will tend to be ever on the lookout for the appearance of this fault in your dog, should you purchase it. That is human nature, and it might be best to keep looking.

If you take a puppy from parents and grandparents that were fit for purpose, willing and biddable, healthy and active – a puppy that looks you in the eye and is affectionate, quiet and gentle – you should have a good chance of success in training it. However, not all of us

are lucky enough to get to know both parents, let alone the grandparents, and this is where pedigrees come in. If there are a number of Field Trial Champions in a working Labrador's pedigree in the first two generations, this bodes well. By and large, a Field Trial Champion has proved he has a good nose, a soft mouth, is silent, bold and trainable. If you can find someone who knows particular dogs in a pedigree and can tell you what they were like, especially when they were young, this indeed will be helpful. In addition, if the sire or dam of your puppy has already produced winning progeny, you should feel quite positive about the puppy's future.

Dog or Bitch?

Bitches are, generally speaking, easier to train than dogs. Most bitches seem better at concentrating. They often have a softer nature and less drive than male dogs. Their main drawback is that they come into season, usually twice a year for three weeks at a time, and during that period they cannot be taken out in public for training or work. It's a very considerate bitch that comes into season at the end of July and the beginning of February! Some people joke that with a bitch you always have an excuse as to why she is not behaving well: she has just been in season, she is just coming into season, or she is halfway between seasons. However, some male dogs seem to be in season all the year round! They can be more wilful than bitches and more easily distracted. That said, many male dogs are willing, affectionate and gentle, but have a vigour that is very eye-catching and exciting to watch.

I have more enquiries for bitches than for dogs. If a person already has a bitch, he will want to keep things simple and have another. However, if he has a dog, he may think he should now have a bitch and mate them in due course and make his money back! I would caution this person with a saying I heard many years ago, 'It's the wise who buy and the fools who breed.' This is so true. If you breed to keep a pup for yourself, you have only, say, seven to choose from, and fewer than that if you want a particular colour or sex. If you buy, you will have hundreds from which to choose.

As regards making your money back, there can be many expenses, both foreseen and unforeseen. Before a mating takes place, both prospective parents should have the health checks for the breed concerned. There are a number of hereditary conditions which can be passed to the next generation, including joint malformations, heart conditions and eye problems. Most whelpings are normal and natural, but if there are complications, the veterinary bills may eat up any profit.

Another aspect of keeping dogs of both sexes is the problem of dealing with matters when the bitch is in season. You will not want to breed with her at every season and even when you do decide to have her mated, you should not leave the two together the whole time or you will not know which date you should expect her to whelp. A bitch in season will upset a dog, and the other dogs in the neighbourhood, for many days, causing them to fret and howl at all hours. Please do think carefully before embarking on this course.

Choice of sex is a matter of personal preference, and as with colour, it is no good going out to buy a blue hat and coming home with a pink one. If you feel you would be more suited to one than to another, stick to your guns.

Colour

Colour choice is principally a matter of personal prefer-ence, but sometimes other factors should be considered. For example, if your shooting is chiefly on the foreshore, it might be best perhaps to choose a yellow dog of a shade that will blend in with the colour of sand and reeds. If your shooting is mainly driven, black might be the best colour. In the shooting field, black Labradors are in the majority, and when someone bursts out, 'Whose dog is that?!' it is sometimes possible to keep secret the ownership of the miscreant!

However, you will seldom successfully override your feelings if you choose a certain colour just because someone else says you should when you know in your heart you prefer another. Believe me, it will affect your attitude to the dog and the results of your training.

AGE OR STAGE OF TRAINING

The Very Young Puppy

I like to have my pups from around seven or eight weeks old. This is when they are starting to learn how to learn. You can't do advanced training, of course, but it is at this age that a pup's first deep impressions are received and he will learn the meanings of voice tone and hand movements and what is expected of him in house, car, garden and kennel. If he gets the wrong impressions at

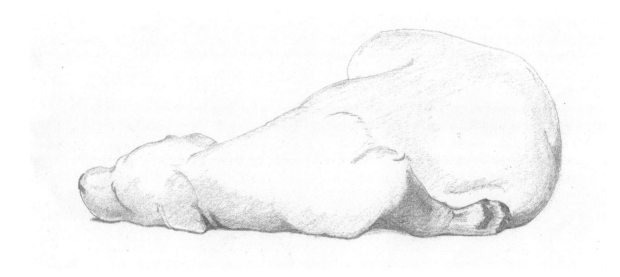

Lotty sleeping.

this age it may be very difficult to reverse his opinions later on. A further advantage to acquiring a very young puppy is that you will have a good chance of bonding with him. You will be able to assess his character and potential before serious training begins.

When choosing a puppy, I always think of going to see litters of Labrador puppies with Mrs Audrey Radclyffe. We usually went when the pups were between four and seven weeks of age. You cannot tell much before the fourth week. She would watch the puppies for a while and then, one by one, she would pick them up. She would hold each puppy up in turn, facing her, to look at its expression, the size of its head and ears, the colour of its eyes. The head and muzzle should be broad and the ears more or less triangular and small-ish, not houndy, and not set on too high or too low. The eyes should be dark and the expression should be kind and steady. In a yellow, she liked to see a good dark pigment of the nose and round the eyes and lips. She would turn the pup to look at the head sideways on, and always liked to see a well defined stop (the differentiation between the level of the muzzle and the top of the head).

Next she would turn its coat back just in front of the flank. She said that if it had a double coat there it would finish with a good coat all over. A short otter-like tail is a must in the Labrador, and the feet should be round and catlike. She would check its teeth to see that it had a scissor bite, i.e. top front incisors just overlapping the lower ones. Then she would let it trot around, noting if it moved sure and straight and whether its toes turned in or out unduly.

Other points she remarked on were whether the puppy looked balanced, in proportion, whether it held its tail too high. Sometimes a puppy will have white toes or a white patch on its chest. 'Sometimes these disappear,' she'd say, and often they do. In any case, a working Labrador will often have mud on its toes, and then, what would it matter?

A well bred Labrador pup, eight weeks old, with a lovely confident expression.

When you are choosing a puppy, you should look for all these points and also make sure there is no umbilical hernia. To do this, let the puppy stand and feel under his tummy, or make him sit like Buddha on your lap. A hernia protrudes like half a pea or larger. Some think these hernias are hereditary, but others believe that most are caused by an over-enthusiastic mother at parturition. Probably there needs to be some inherent weakness in that area for the enthusiasm to cause a hernia. Some do close up by themselves; some need surgical attention. Your veterinary surgeon will advise you.

At seven or eight weeks you should be able to detect by feeling if a male puppy has both its testicles descended. If one or both testicles have been retained

Puppy lying on his back on my lap, calm and acquiescent.

within the body, this could lead to trouble later in life. Again, a veterinary surgeon can advise you.

Temperament is difficult to assess in a very young puppy, beyond noticing whether he is bold or retiring, quiet or noisy. It is always helpful if you can see one or both parents, particularly the mother. Remember the saying, 'Breeding will out!' The temperament of the parents can be an indication of how the pup may eventually develop, but environment plays a very important part too. For example, a highly strung breeder can infect a puppy with the same trait. The most important phase of socialization in a puppy's life takes place between four and fourteen weeks and it is remarkable

how strongly a puppy can be influenced during this period.

Ask the breeder if you may have a low chair to sit on so that you can watch the puppies from a comfortable vantage point. I like to do a couple of little tests on puppies I am considering purchasing, but am careful to ask the breeder if he or she minds. I lay a puppy on its back on my lap to see if it will accept this without struggling. A little struggle is all right, but an absolute refusal to lie happily is not good, as it is supposed to indicate a stubborn, resistant nature. This would not be helpful in later training. Extreme nervousness can show in this little test too. However, puppies change from day to day, and one which seems nervous on Monday may be quite calm and happy on Wednesday. Some

Puppy showing the retrieving instinct: he sees the prize…

breeders may object to you doing something which they may perceive as stressful to their puppies, but this little test can and should be done very gently.

At five weeks, it is possible to discover if a puppy has the retrieving instinct. The test for this has to be done with one puppy at a time, so you will have to ask the breeder if you can separate the pup you want to test from the others for a minute or two. Tape up a matchbox which has a few matches in it. Shake this to attract the puppy's attention, then throw it a little way from him. If he runs out, picks up the box and turns round in his tracks, he has the retrieving instinct. The main thing you want to see is that

he turns round when he has picked up the box. Don't despair if he shows no interest in it, or runs off with it. That may be Monday; on Wednesday he may well do it in 'copy book' fashion.

I like to see a nice tail action, one where the tail swishes back and forth, often slapping the ribs on either side with each sweep. It's a lovely sight. When a dog is working, it is the tail that tells you what the nose is finding out. Style is shown mainly in the tail action. A stylish dog is one which looks purposeful and is a pleasure to watch.

He starts off for it…

LEFT: The pick-up...

BELOW: The crucial part: he turns...

RIGHT: *On his way back…*

BELOW: *A little resistance…*

On he comes...

He decides to play...

The delivery.

*Eight-month-old
Labrador asleep,*

The Older Pup

If the pup is not acquired at between seven and twelve weeks, there is something to be said for leaving it until the age of six or eight months, as between the fourth and sixth month the pup will be teething. He will find it difficult to concentrate, and retrieving should be left entirely alone. During this time he will go through many changes, both in personality and in looks. He may be quite the delinquent or exhibit worrying nervousness.

A youngster of nine months.

His appearance may cause concern, too. His ears may 'fly' – stick up at a funny angle – and he may look odd in other ways, and it is not fair to decide at this stage what he will look like later, as these things often correct themselves after teething. At six months he is ready to start more serious training, as he can concentrate for longer periods and is beginning to mature physically.

A youngster of this age is often available because the owner or breeder has started off running two puppies together. It is easier to have two than one, if you have the facilities. Then at a later date, you can make a more informed choice than you can with a little pup, and part with the one you prefer less. This youngster will effectively be second pick of litter and there may be nothing wrong with it other than perhaps it is a little slower, or bigger or smaller, or carries its tail too high.

Try to choose the animal whose temperament complements, rather than contrasts with, your own character – and perhaps most importantly, find one which looks you in the face.

Over six months, the pup will be developing his own personality and doggy habits and becoming sexually mature. If he has been well socialized – taken about in the car, brought into the house, meeting lots of other people and dogs, and exercised under control, never allowed more than forty yards from the handler – your training will probably be sopped up like water into a sponge. The dog will be delighted to have new interests in his life.

However, if he has been kept in a kennel alone, it is possible that he will be timid and shy, be ignorant of the meanings of voice tone and hand movement, or be extremely boisterous and excitable, with none of the good manners of a 'home-reared' puppy. See how he responds to the 'muzzle-holding technique' (*see* Chapter 4) – if he is acquiescent, do not be afraid to proceed; if he resists it vigorously, give him a few moments to get to know you better and try it again, and if he still struggles against you, I would recommend you look at another pup.

If he has been kennelled with another dog and not properly socialized, he will be what I call 'dog-minded' as opposed to 'people-minded', preferring canine company (and instruction) and missing it noisily for nights on end when he is kennelled alone! This is not a reason to discard the dog out of hand – it just means that some remedial training is needed. Again, apply the muzzle-holding technique and assess his response.

Having Two Puppies at Once

It can be easier in some ways to have two puppies instead of just one. Taking one pup away from his litter-mates to a solitary life does have its down side. The puppy will never have known life without his mother or siblings and, unless he was an only pup, he will always have had company. Of course he will be upset when left alone for the first time, and unless he is given the confidence that you will return, he may go on being upset and very noisy, and perhaps destructive, for some time.

Two pups together, even if they are not from the same litter, will settle happily very quickly. They will encourage each other to eat well, and they will supply warmth and companionship for one another. They can be very rough in play! However, you must treat them as individuals right from the start. Give each of them some one-to-one quality time every day. Teach them the ground rules individually, such as not to be noisy or chew their bed. Feed them in separate bowls, and make sure they do not swap.

Later you need to be self-disciplined: either you part with one when they are no more than six months old, or you start their training, separately. You must take each one out by himself.

The Trained Dog

If you opt for a trained Labrador, be sure to have it demonstrated away from its usual training ground. It should be confident and obedient to its handler. Ascertain beforehand that you will see the dog's reaction to a shotgun being fired. Take some form of cold game with you – a pheasant, partridge or duck, or a woodcock if you can arrange it. Many dogs are reluctant to pick woodcock.

You should already know what a trained dog should be capable of before going to see a dog demonstrated. If you are unsure, ask a knowledgeable friend to go with you. Ask to see the dog retrieve seen and unseen

Two puppies will play together and keep each other company.

dummies or game, see if it will jump reasonable obstacles on command, and enter water willingly and bring the retrieve to hand without dropping it to shake. You will be able to learn the handler's signals and commands, but just to be on the safe side, if you are genuinely interested, go through them with the handler and make notes in order to be sure. You should be able to have several demonstrations so that you really get to know the dog. Ideally, if it is the shooting season, you should be able to see the dog working at a shoot.

I like purchasers of my trained dogs to come back after two or three weeks for a refresher course to make sure the dog is maintaining his peak level of training, and that the handler is realizing the dog's full capabilities.

Every dog has its faults, and hopefully you will be honest with yourself and decide if what you see is truly what you want, and also, if the faults you notice are ones which are innate, like whining, and not correctible, or training faults which could with time be rectified.

HEALTH CONCERNS

Health is obviously an important issue where a gundog is concerned, and your Labrador needs to be sound, both mentally and physically. This means of course that, amongst other things, he should be active, athletic, have stamina, good eyesight and a confident demeanour.

The overall impression that a healthy puppy or dog should give is one of cleanness and brightness: clean coat, eyes, ears, nose, teeth, skin, genitals; bright eyes and personality. In addition his feet should be neat, with pads that are not splayed and the nails evenly worn. The teeth should have a close scissor bite in front, the lower incisors closing just behind the upper.

There should be no sign of rash, and no bald patches. Evidence that the dog scratches a lot may show as an area of broken-ended hair behind the shoulders, and this could indicate a number of skin conditions. Gummy eyes can be a very bad sign, and head-shaking can mean mites in the ears. The dog may not shake his head while he is out with his handler and you, because he is so interested in everything else, but a tell-tale sign is that the tips of his ears are bare and sometimes bloody because he has hit them on things when he was shaking his head earlier indoors.

Certain symptoms can mean either a serious chronic problem or an easily rectified one, so it is wise to call in an expert – by which I mean your veterinary surgeon. For example, bare, wet patches could be due simply to an allergy to flea bites. If the dog and his environment are kept free of fleas, the skin will clear and the coat will grow back. However, the cause could be mange or ringworm, both of which are fairly serious problems and not easy to diagnose even with a skin test.

So you see, without an expert opinion you could turn down a very useful dog because you are wary of certain symptoms which might be easily eradicated. Conversely, you could ignore or miss a point which could be the cause of endless future trouble and expense to you.

You should never buy a dog or puppy because you feel sorry for it unless you are happy to be taking on what may be a lifetime of problems.

When you first take your new puppy or dog to the veterinary surgeon, explain the purpose for which he is intended so that he can be checked for all the relevant points.

The overall impression a healthy puppy or dog should give is one of cleanness and brightness.

Nowadays, both parents of any dog or puppy you are considering purchasing should have been tested for the hereditary diseases that occur in the breed. Before deciding to buy, you should have seen the pertinent certificates. Each parent should have a current clear eye certificate. Both parents should have good hip and elbow scores. Dysplasia has been a problem in the Labrador breed for many years. Dysplasia means malformation, not displacement as some people think. No one knows for sure how hip and elbow dysplasia are inherited, but it follows that if you put the best to the best and hope for the best, this is the best you can do. So choosing a puppy from parents with good scores is a good point at which to start (there will be more on this in Chapter 4 under 'Exercise'). Just recently, researchers have begun work to try to establish a DNA test that will show how hip and elbow dysplasia are inherited.

In my opinion, a score of zero to seven or eight for hips (each side) is acceptable in Labradors, the lower being the better. I believe the breed mean (average) score is 15, being the total of the scores for both hips. Elbows are scored from zero to three, each side, zero being normal. If the dog you are thinking of acquiring is aged over a year, he may have had his eyes checked and his hips and elbows scored. The price will reflect this. A nice natured, well bred, fully trained dog will be in the four-figure price range, so if you are buying such a dog, he certainly should have these certificates.

HOW MUCH SHOULD YOU PAY?

Prices alter with time so I will give you some idea by using a comparison. A well bred Labrador puppy – that is, a puppy with a working pedigree with lots of red ink, meaning Field Trial Champions, in its pedigree – should be priced at about three times the amount of a good class of shooting jacket. This will vary a bit according to the region – puppies from the Home Counties tend to be dearer than ones from the North Country and Scotland.

Puppies that are not Kennel Club registered but have a good working pedigree are usually half the price of registered pups. You should not pay a very high price if the pedigree includes more than one show-bred grandparent.

To my mind, the price of a puppy aged over four months of age should be about £100 per month of life above the puppy price. This rate of increase goes on as time passes and training progresses.

If the dog has won a trial, another rise in price may be added. If he is a young Field Trial Champion, with good hips, elbows and eyes, he should fetch a price that reflects this, bearing in mind his potential as a stud dog. There are now several DNA tests which can be done to indicate whether a dog carries certain hereditary conditions, and you may find that your prospective purchase has had some or all of these tests done. With all this in mind, you must still be truly satisfied with the answer to the question, 'Why is he for sale?'

Price can be affected by many other factors such as temperament, size, colour, coat quality and looks. It is a good thing to ask for advice from someone you trust – and of course, like anything else, only you can decide what you are prepared to pay.

Free to a Good Home

You will sometimes hear of dogs aged ten to twelve months old being offered 'free to good home'. Beware: there is usually some problem. The dog may be noisy, aggressive, bad with children or other dogs, an unbeatable escapologist, incurable chewer, thief or carpet wetter. Sometimes, to be fair, dogs advertised in this way are available for genuine reasons, such as a death in the family or the circumstances of the owner, and not due to any fault in the dog.

If you go to see such a dog, take a few biscuits in your pocket. If you like the look of the dog and it is the sex and colour you had decided upon and not overly shy or noisy, try a few tests. Ask someone to go into the next room and burst a blown-up paper bag or slam a big book shut, while you watch the dog's reactions. If all goes well, try it in the same room. If he tolerates this noise well, there is a good chance that he will not be gun-nervous. Throw a tennis ball, rolled-up sock or leather glove: if he will go and pick it up, good; if he brings it back, so much the better. If he has a decent pedigree and is registered, you will start to be quite interested.

As a further test, ask if you may take the dog for a walk, on lead. The biscuits should help with this. Its reactions to you, other people, other dogs, noises and so on, will tell you a lot about its character. If it seems sensible and pays attention when you speak to it, and if it is friendly and looks at you, I think you may feel confident in taking it on. Only time will tell if it is clean indoors, does not chew or steal, and does not open doors and windows, but these are things which can be got round or rectified.

Occasionally an older, fully trained dog may become available at, say, the age of eight or nine years. He or she may be a retired field trial winner, or she may be a brood bitch which has had her quota of puppies. A nominal price may or may not be charged – often the owner just hopes to find a good retirement home for the dog where he or she will have some shooting work. The drawback with such a dog is that its working life is limited. You will have to be aware that the time is approaching where the dog will have to be paced – they seldom pace themselves – and it will gradually need more care and attention than a young dog.

You should say that you would like your veterinary surgeon to check the dog over before you make a final decision, and you may even be able to persuade the owner to let you have the dog on trial for a week or two which has its obvious advantages, one of which is to see how it behaves in unfamiliar surroundings. This sounds like looking a gift horse in the mouth but time is valuable and if this dog is merely pet quality, you need to know. It must be a good thing to be wary and to find out as much as possible about the dog.

WHAT YOU SHOULD COME HOME WITH

As well as the puppy or dog, you should be given the Kennel Club Registration Certificate – make sure the breeder or registered owner has signed it on the back. You should also be given a copy of the dog's pedigree. If the pedigree is handwritten, spelling may be difficult to decipher but do not be too concerned – as long as the dog is registered, and you are happy that the papers are supplied in good faith, you can obtain a printed, certified pedigree from the Kennel Club. In addition, if appropriate, you should receive the dog's inoculation certificate and any hip, elbow and eye certificates. Ask if you may have a few days' supply of the food the dog is used to, and the dates of the most recent worm and skin parasite treatment, also the name of the products used.

Understandably, if you are purchasing from someone who does not know you, they may wish to withhold the paperwork until your cheque has cleared. Of course, you should be shown all the papers to make sure that all is in order, and you must make sure you have given your full address so that the papers can be posted on to you. If you pay by cash, the vendor should hand you all the papers. Paying by cheque gives you the advantage of time in which to have your veterinary surgeon check the dog over, and if there is any consequent disaccord with the vendor, the cheque can be stopped and the dog returned.

In the case of the trained dog, you must be sure that you have the same whistle that he has been trained on, and you must have a 'concert' with the trainer to make sure you have the way of blowing it right. You should also make a written note of the commands he has been trained to, with their meanings.

TO SUM UP

I think it is accurate to say that you will seldom see the best dogs advertised. The best pups are booked before they are born, or they and well trained dogs are quickly sold by word of mouth. However, there are many well bred animals available from less celebrated kennels, usually at less elevated prices. You just have to make enquiries and keep on until you find what you are looking for. Contact someone you trust and ring the numbers they give you; one call will lead to another until you come upon something promising.

You can often tell when speaking to a person, even on the telephone, whether they are genuine or not. If something sounds fishy, it probably is. No one will tell you the whole truth, but you can usually read between the lines. If the vendor tells you the dog's faults, be careful that you do not take it on as a sort of challenge. You will probably be sorry. There are seldom circumstances where an owner will part with his best dog, so you must be satisfied as to why the dog is for sale. 'Let the buyer beware' was never truer than with livestock.

Another factor which may influence you is feeling sorry for a dog. If a dog appears to be afraid of his owner or will not come to him, you may pity the dog and want to remove it from that situation. It is difficult to advise you because your wish to 'rescue' the dog may be strong. You may have a long road of rehabilitation ahead of you and you may make a huge success of things – but equally you may be buying a pack of trouble, and spend lots of money and lots of time to no avail. The dog just might be a complete rogue or a nervous wreck and you will be wasting your time, money and energy. Sometimes it is better simply to harden your heart.

At any rate, if you are not happy in any important point, do not act in haste. Take time to think it over, go and see other dogs and puppies, go back to the ones you liked for a second or even third look. This acquisition could last you for twelve or more years. It is a big investment in time and money. There is also the not inconsiderable matter of emotional attachment that usually comes into the equation.

Finally, having found a dog which is bred for work, whose breed, age, stage of training, temperament, colour and sex suit your circumstances, make sure that you actually like the dog and that he or she seems to like you.

CHAPTER 2

GETTING OFF TO A GOOD START

BEFORE COLLECTING THE NEWCOMER

First of all you should ask the vendor if you can come early in the day to fetch your new acquisition. This is so that the dog or puppy will have the largest part of the day to get used to his new owner and surroundings before nightfall. Arrange to collect him early even if you have a long journey to get there, and equally home: this is an investment for the future.

A day or two before you fetch your dog or puppy, ask the vendor to put a few sheets of newspaper in his bed. Putting this paper in with him when you collect him will help him to feel at home. Alternatively, you could ask the vendor to give you a piece of blanket or a towel with which the dog is familiar. It will be helpful to have someone with you when you are collecting a puppy, either to drive or to keep an eye on him while you drive. If you have the pup on your lap, you will soon be sorry and so will he – you will both become

A suitable cage in which to keep a Labrador puppy out of harm's way in the house or car.

far too hot. He really would be better in a cage. Make the cage comfortable, and put in it the paper or bedding the vendor has given you.

A few minutes spent in getting him used to the cage before you leave his old home will be time well spent. Have some biscuits ready. Show him the cage and open the door. Throw in a biscuit and hopefully he will go in after it. Some puppies will not go in voluntarily so you will have to lift them in. Do so firmly but not roughly. The pup will then be able to reach the biscuit in the box, but give him another one before he is allowed out. Do not shut the door, but let him out or call him out straightaway. Repeat this procedure several times, eventually shutting the door behind him. Give him another biscuit through the wire, then open the door and let him out. In this way you give him a good association with going into and being in the cage. He learns that it is not permanent – the door does open and he will be allowed out. Each time you put him in and close the door behind him, leave him in for a little bit longer. Only give him a biscuit when he is inside the cage, not when he is out of it.

When he will stay quietly in the cage for ten seconds, go out of sight for a few seconds, return, give him a biscuit and let him out. Repeat this a few times, gradually lengthening the time that you are out of his sight – by this means you will probably be able to drive home without him screaming and yelling.

If you are collecting an older pup or an adult dog, a cage is again the best way of transporting him. Accustom him to the cage in the same way as a puppy. (There is more about cages in Chapter 4.)

Before you go to fetch the new puppy or dog, it is a good idea to collect your thoughts so as to avoid making mistakes, as far as is possible, right at the beginning. Prepare yourself by thinking of how the dog is going to see things – for example, he may not have consciously ever heard your voice before, may never have been in a car or house, may never have been without canine company. You want him to have a good impression of you, and pleasant associations with your hands and voice. Resolve to think before acting, and try to see why he does what he does.

Prepare a place for him that he can call his own. Have a dish for him, a water bowl and a supply of food. Perhaps the previous owner will give you some of the food he has been fed, or you could ask beforehand what it is so that you can purchase some of the same in advance. This is an important point because, first, having familiar food will help him to settle, and secondly, a sudden change in diet could upset his digestion and cause him to make a mess when he would not have otherwise. This would not be a good start.

His place could be a kennel or a basket under the kitchen table or a cage in a convenient corner. Whatever you arrange, make it dry and comfortable, easy to keep clean, and out of everyone's way. When you bring the puppy into your home, let him see you put his own newspaper, towel or bedding in his bed. It will smell of him and his old home, and should help him to accept the new place.

Another thing that can be done to relieve a puppy of his feelings of separation and loneliness is to put a hot-water bottle in his bed. It should be one of the old-fashioned stone sort, and should be wrapped in a towel or a padded pillowcase. The water should be hot but not boiling. Some people like to put a ticking clock with a pup – this is to simulate the heartbeat of his missing siblings – but it must be in a tin or box so that the puppy cannot destroy it and perhaps eat some of the pieces.

Indoors, the oval padded beds with sides to keep off draughts and a tough, water-resistant surface are good as they are light, comfortable, washable and easily taken wherever you want the dog to go. My dogs travel many miles a year with me, sometimes sleeping in the car or in friends' houses or hotel rooms. They know that where their bed is, is their own place. Moisture from the dog's body can collect under the bed but if it is put out in the sun to dry periodically or rests on a sheet of cardboard, the problem is overcome. There are also rigid plastic kidney-shaped beds in which you can place VetBed, one of the greatest inventions of the last century. VetBed is an artificial fleece material which comes in a variety of colours and is easily washed and dried. It is fairly expensive but lasts for years and years and dogs seem to like lying on it. Most of these plastic beds now have ventilation slots in the bottom which stop moisture collecting.

In the kennel, VetBed can be destroyed because

A four-month-old pup in the cage. She can stand up, turn round and lie down. She has bedding, water, and toys and bones to amuse her.

dogs are not supervised as they are in the house. For kennel bedding, I use newspaper torn into strips as the best of a lot of bad ideas. It blows about a bit, but smells seem to be neutralized by it to a degree. Shredded paper blows about much too readily, straw and hay harbour parasites and dust, and shavings become dusty, which can irritate a dog's eyes; furthermore if shavings are wetted by dogs they smell really disgusting. Blankets need to be changed often to keep them dry, and dogs like to chew them and often pieces are swallowed, which can cause a blockage in the gut.

NOTES ON NAMES

Your dog or puppy should be registered and will therefore have a registered name, but you don't need to call him by this name. He may already have a 'call name', and if you like it and it is sensible and unlike any of the words you intend to use for his training, it is fine to stick to that. If, however, you do not like the name his former owner has been using, it is easy to change it and probably a good idea – not least because there is always a chance you will permanently dislike the name, and it may have repercussions with regard to your general attitude to the dog and thus your training.

Some people think it is bad luck to change an animal's name and you must decide for yourself how you feel about that. If you do decide to change a dog's name, choose the name you want and never call him his old name again. Use the new name at every opportunity: when you call him, feed him, let him in or out, pat or reward him – he will take to the new name in a day. Over time, you will possibly, as I do, give him nicknames, and you will be surprised at how many names a dog will recognize and respond to.

I do not like the use of human names for my dogs, if only because of the possible embarrassment if I were speaking angrily to 'Max' only to find that that was my host's name and he was within earshot. I usually choose two-syllable names, and I prefer names that have two meanings – for example, 'Caper' for a lively black dog. That's just my bit of fun! My one exception to the human name rule was when I called a very favourite puppy 'Lottie'. This was after a very favourite Aunt Lottie who had a sweet nature and a mind as sharp as a tack, and still went into the office, and worked efficiently, well into her nineties. Her namesake followed her closely in that she had a lovely temperament and a quick mind, and still worked efficiently and well until nearly fifteen years of age.

It's rather like superstition, but I dislike a name with connotations of hardness, roughness or sharpness. I would not, for instance, call a Labrador 'Rock', or 'Hawk', or 'Thorn', or 'Viper', or even 'Bramble'.

I once called a dog 'Scout' which of course sounds like 'Out', so when I said, 'Scout, in,' he decided he would prefer to be out, and chose not to go in. When it dawned on me what was happening, I changed his name to 'Nimbus' and by the end of the day all was well.

You will encounter similar problems if you choose names containing 'No,' such as 'Bruno', 'Beano', 'Juno', 'Domino', 'Minnow' and 'Noah'. As a result the scold word 'No' will have a mixed meaning and will be devalued. 'No!' should stand alone and have a clear meaning for when you really need it. A similar case can be made against the names 'Sinbad', as it contains the word

'bad', and 'Oban' – this sounds like 'No, bad' – and 'Paddock' or even 'Paddy' can sound like 'bad dog'!

It is best to avoid names which sound like commands. 'Teal' and 'Seal' can still be all right as long as you use another word, such as 'Close' instead of 'Heel'. 'Bright' and 'Flight' can be confused with 'Right' or 'All right' if you happen to use these words with your dog. 'Kay', 'Fay' and 'Tay' are like 'Okay' which we say all day, every day without even hearing ourselves say it. Remember that most of us say 'All right' and 'Right' as often as we say 'Okay'.

A dog called 'Boy' came to me for training some years ago. All dogs are called 'Boy' and he knew it, so when it suited, he ignored it. I managed to persuade the owner to change it. Once again the name 'Nimbus' was given – problem solved.

If you already have a dog, make sure you choose a name for the newcomer that has a completely different sound. If, for example, you have Dollar and Dolly, both dogs will eventually ignore their own name when it suits them.

There is a growing trend of sending a dog on his name alone for a seen retrieve, and indeed, I do this. The idea is that the dog does not take his eye off the fall and nor do you. However, if your dog's name begins with 'S' or the 'S' sound it could cause a problem. I have a dog called Cedar, which is a nice name, but I ran into trouble when a dummy was thrown in a puppy test, and I was asked to leave the dog sitting and retrieve the dummy by hand. I said 'Sit', but he heard the first hiss of his name and was off like a flash. I realized my mistake, and from that time on I used the word 'Hup' instead of 'Sit' for him.

WHEN YOU GET HOME

Whatever you do when you arrive home, do not let the puppy or dog loose unless you are in a dog-proof and fairly small area. In the case of a puppy, it is best to lift him out and carry him to an area where he cannot run under the car, somewhere with grass so he can sniff around and perhaps spend his first pennies while you are there with him, on grass, this being a good habit to encourage. I use the command 'Hurry up' for this, which is a good phrase because the dog will soon come to know what it means, but other people will not. Once a dog associates the act with the command he will perform quickly, saving you from having to hang around outside for ages on rainy evenings.

The older dog should be put on a lead before he is let out of the car. He can then be taken on a short tour of his new territory, and you can begin the team-mate-making process in that you are touring with him, showing him around.

Occasionally you will come across a youngster which has never been on the lead, and in this case you will only frighten him by putting him on a lead in this new, strange place, and long-term damage may be done. You should establish before you purchase him whether he is used to being on a lead, and if not, you should take a flat, buckle-on collar with you when you go to collect him. Put it on him before you put him in the car, and by the time you arrive home, he should have forgotten the initial ticklishness and newness of the collar and you can attach a lead. At least you can then take hold of him to prevent him jumping straight out of the car when you open the door, which is better and safer than grabbing him by the scruff. Do not, however, then get into the situation where you are playing him like a fish on a line and terrifying him: take your time, allow the lead as much slack as possible, and coax him and bribe him until he is in an enclosed area, somewhere safe to be let free. Follow your instincts – you may be able to take the lead off, or you may consider it prudent to leave it trailing so you can be sure of catching him again.

After a short while, take him to where his bed or indoor cage is and, putting the newspaper from the car in it, invite him to go into it. Use a treat as before, and then let him come out. Let him watch you prepare his food, make him sit and remain sitting while you put it down, then say, 'Paid for,' and indicate that he may eat. This is all good bonding stuff.

He may be too unsettled to eat, however, even if you leave him alone. After ten minutes, whether he has eaten some of it or none, pick up the bowl and put it away. In the case of a puppy, you can offer it to him again in an hour. In the case of the older dog, shut him away for ten minutes, then take him out for a short walk. On return, offer him the food again. After

ten minutes, take up the bowl and do not offer it again until the next meal time. By doing this, you will increase his hunger and eventually his appetite should induce him to eat.

The first time you leave him, he may kick up a fuss. Go to him and say, 'Be quiet,' in a normal voice, and at the same moment splash a little water in his face. A water pistol is good as you only want a little water in the right place. If he is in a cage and the water doesn't deter him, repeat 'Be quiet', take a rolled-up newspaper and whack the cage once with it. Then leave the room, saying 'Be quiet' in a normal but firm voice, shut the door and immediately open it again and go back to him. If he is quiet, say 'Be quiet' in a normal voice and give him a small titbit. Have a container of them handy. If he has already begun to make a racket, say 'Be quiet' in a firm, but not loud, voice and repeat the whack and the rest of the performance again. It takes time and much repetition for a dog to realize the connection between his noise-making, your command and the splash or whack, but eventually, if you are determined and consistent, the penny will drop. Keep your voice normal – raising it can be interpreted by the dog as you joining in. Make your absence very short – your aim is to return before he starts to make a noise so that you can reward him for being quiet. Once he realizes he will be given a treat for quietness, you can begin to slowly extend the time you are out of sight.

This treatment may seem to you to be a bit hard on the dog when he has had such a huge change in his life, but it comes under the heading of, 'Start off as you mean to go on'. You must be consistent with dogs. If you are not, they will soon realize that it is worth looking for the loopholes in your resolve, and they will be constantly testing you. This is not the way to gain reliable obedience and co-operation.

If you can get out of the room and back again without the pup making a noise, however short your absence may have been, praise him lavishly. Sometimes give him a treat, but not every time. Never be nice to him if he is being noisy – if you are, he will quickly train you to return to him by making a noise every time you leave the room.

If you leave a dog or puppy to 'cry himself out', he may eventually abandon his noise-making, but the

Quality time – a five-month-old pup and handler getting to know each other.

chances are that he may not. My method shows him quickly that he has a choice: to be noisy and attract an unpleasant reaction from me, or to be calm and quiet and receive kindness and reward.

During the day and in the evening, give the new dog or puppy some quality time. Sit with him and let him get to know you and the other people with whom he is going to live. You could do this anywhere comfortable – sitting on a bench or on a wall in the sun, or perhaps by the fire in the living room – anywhere where the two of you, and perhaps other members of your family, can spend some quiet time bonding with him. Just sitting with, and talking to your new dog, grooming, playing with or just fondling him, will be time well spent. He is going to be a valuable companion to you, so it is a good thing to build a friendship with him. Try to do this for a few minutes every day.

Last thing before bedtime, about 10pm, take him outdoors so that he can spend his pennies. Remember to say 'Hurry up', and praise him sincerely when he does what he should. When you come in again, put him in his place with the newspaper from his old home, give him a toy and a biscuit, make sure he has water, and tell him to settle down and then leave him. The space he has should be fairly restricted, because the more room he has to move around in, the more likely he is to soil his surroundings. If he is noisy, go through the procedure as above. Don't just leave him hoping he will give up – some dogs just will not give up – but return to him and make it plain that you will not tolerate unnecessary noise, that making a noise brings unpleasant, physical consequences.

A FEW WORDS ABOUT TOYS

There is an amazing array of toys on the market which are safe and enjoyable for dogs to amuse themselves with, and, usually, to try to destroy. The good safe ones are quite expensive. An important consideration when choosing a shop toy is that it is probably not a good idea for it to have a squeak. A squeak will make the puppy chew the toy, and who can say that this won't make a dog hard-mouthed? I'd rather not take the risk. A solution, of course, is to undo the stitching, take out the squeaker, and sew it up again.

Young dogs need interesting things to do – they can't be expected to sleep all day, and you can't spend the whole day pandering to them and amusing them. The playthings you give a puppy or dog must be, above all, safe. As a general rule, things made of cardboard or plastic are expendable, although it must be remembered that much of a car's interior may be made of plastic! I collect all the rigid plastic and cardboard household packaging – cereal boxes, milk cartons, yoghurt pots, cream and ice cream containers, and so on – and give them to my puppies to play with. I do not wash them – the pups do that – but I do cut the cup-shaped pots and the plastic milk bottles in half, vertically. This is especially important where the small pots are concerned as puppies can and do put their snouts right in to lick out the remains, and I have known them, when very young, not be able to work out how to remove the cup from their face. This is a recipe for suffocation. I once had a puppy get his head stuck in a six-inch length of five-inch diameter poly-pipe. He was unable to extricate himself, and I had great difficulty in removing it. It had seemed beforehand to be such a safe thing with which to play – how wrong I was! All these recycled 'toys' are free, but they do make the kennel, run, garden or house untidy.

Some people say that puppies should not have toys. If there is more than one puppy, they will learn to steal the toys from each other, which invariably involves a firm grip, much tugging and sometimes a scrap. In theory, this could lead to hard mouth. Also, a dog which has snatched toys from one of its littermates may think it is all right to snatch the retrieve from other dogs when he is older. I have found that they do this instinctively anyway, even in the case of an only puppy. All I can say is that I have always given my puppies toys, and not one, in all these years, has grown up to be hard-mouthed on game. Two developed a hard mouth on runners, after having been clawed by lively cock pheasants, but that is another story. After all, dogs have the instinct to chase, bite, tear at and eat prey, but a mother dog will carry a puppy without damaging it. Circumstances alter cases – a dog is capable of behaving differently in different situations. Almost all well bred Labradors will carry a retrieve gently, but will still chew and eat their food. Snatching things

A collection of 'toys' suitable for puppies to play with and chew.

from other dogs is an instinctive thing. As with other instinctive things, we know that a dog can be trained to resist an instinct and not snatch things from another dog.

INTRODUCING THE NEW PUP TO A RESIDENT DOG

If you already have another dog, and let's assume it's an adult, you should be diplomatic in introducing the newcomer, especially if they are to share the same quarters. Take the older dog with you when you go to collect the puppy, and introduce them on the puppy's turf. The older dog may be playful or indifferent, but usually adults growl at puppies and try to get away from them. At worst, he or she may be quite aggressive towards the pup. Make sure to take some small treats in your pocket and give one to the puppy and then one to the older dog. Make sure it is puppy first, adult second. Do this three or four times and the older dog should start to think that the pup is the cause of the bounty. Only put them together to travel if you are absolutely certain the adult is friendly towards the pup; you don't want the pup to be scarred physically or mentally in its first association with you and the dog already in situ.

The new pup is tolerated by the resident dog.

At home, do not leave the two unsupervised unless you are certain that all is well. Better to err on the side of caution if you have the least doubt. This is another situation where a cage is worth every penny of its cost.

Whenever you feed the pup, give the older dog a tiny amount in his own bowl. Soon he will begin to look upon the newcomer as good news. Put down the puppy's food first – this will raise the puppy in the older dog's estimation. You might think it would make the older dog jealous, but the effect is almost the opposite: it shows the older dog that you hold the puppy in esteem, and provided the existing dog regards you as pack leader, he will take this as a sign that he should show the pup a degree of respect.

Always remember that the puppy's exercise must be carefully monitored, and do not allow the two dogs to play unsupervised, or for more than a few minutes at a time.

THE FIRST NIGHT

After you have settled the new puppy or dog for the night at, say, 11pm, you will hope that he will be all right until the morning. This is probably not to be. After the house has gone quiet, he may make some noise. Perhaps he needs to spend a penny. You should take him outside and say 'Hurry up', and hopefully he will perform. If he obviously does not need to 'go', put him back indoors with a biscuit or chew, and leave him. If he does need to empty himself, he will, and you can reward him with a biscuit and take him indoors. Once he has done his business, he really has no reason to be noisy apart from loneliness, and while you may be sympathetic, you must resist rewarding him for being upset. With a very young puppy you may have to go to him in the small hours to take him out so he can relieve himself. Apart from this, be determined, more so than he is. Scold for noise, praise for quiet: you will succeed in the end because he will finally realize that he comes to no harm on his own and you will eventually come back to him.

THE NEXT DAY

Go down early next morning, say at about 5.30 or 6am. With any luck he will have been able to stay clean. Take him outdoors straightaway to spend his pennies, remembering to say 'Hurry up'. When he has performed, he can be given his breakfast. After this, he should go out again briefly, then be put in his bed for the food to settle. There are five things that make a puppy need to empty his bladder or bowel: waking up, eating, excitement, exercise and fear. In the case of eating, of course, it is not the meal he is eating that is to be excreted; the act of eating stimulates the gut and that makes him need to 'go'. You may find it helpful to set a timer to go off every half hour or so in order to take him outdoors when necessary. Most small puppies seem to need to spend a penny every half hour during the day, and to do a poo about four to six times in twenty-four hours.

At about 11 o'clock, take him out for a short run and a few minutes' training. You should have a plan as to what exercises you would like to do with him – see chapters 6, 7 and 8. Make sure you choose fairly simple exercises so that all goes well. After six minutes, maximum, end the session on a good note and put him away in his quiet place for a while.

The puppy will need his lunch around midday, followed by an outing to do his business, then a rest.

In the afternoon, you could take a grown dog for a walk, probably not for more than half an hour, just to acquaint him with your district and to further your friendship with him. Before you let him free, you will have to be certain that he will not run away, so you should only let him off the lead in a dog-proof area in the early days. After a week or two you will sense how much you can trust him – but always err on the side of caution.

With a youngster under ten months, a ten-minute run five or six times a day in familiar surroundings will be adequate (see Chapter 3, Exercise).

Supper can be given after this outing or later, and the little puppy will possibly need a fourth meal late in the evening. My dogs are never fed at an exact time – I don't want them looking at their watches and telling me that their meal is late!

CHAPTER 3

PERTINENT CARE

A Labrador needs to be fit and healthy in order to perform his job. There are many very thorough treatises on the care and feeding of dogs: this chapter is aimed specifically at helping you to attain and maintain peak fitness in your working Labrador.

FEEDING

Early Days

A puppy has only one chance of making the growth to last all his life, so the quality of the food that you give him should be the best that you can afford – though always bearing in mind that Labrador puppies should not grow too quickly. Some of the modern complete puppy foods are too nourishing, and feeding these very high protein, high oil foods can be like force-feeding pigs for early slaughter: they are like rocket fuel, when all the puppy needs is good quality food and a well balanced diet in order to produce good quality, well balanced growth. I recommend the complete puppy and junior foods of no more than 28 per cent protein and 18 per cent oil. The foods in the middle price range are fine for Labrador puppies, and there is no need to feed vitamin or mineral supplements with these foods.

Of course, the natural food of dogs is meat, but it is not just meat, it is the whole animal. When dogs, wild or otherwise, catch prey, they eat the gut content and entrails, the fur or feathers, bone, sinews and cartilage as well as the meat. I sometimes wonder if anyone has ever done an analysis of a whole rabbit or pheasant in the way that an analysis is done of the complete foods. I imagine that this has been done and that both might come out at the same or similar levels. Then the chief difference would be that one is fresh and the other is dry and processed, and that some of the ingredients are substitutes for parts of the diet naturally found by a dog. For example, a dog could eat a whole blackbird that might have ingested beetles and earthworms, berries and seeds. A dog food manufacturer would not put these delicacies into his feed, nor would he include the whole skeleton, or the hair, scales or feathers of the herbivores whose meat is traditionally used in dog foods. He would substitute with such things as bone meal, poultry and fish meat meal, minerals and vitamins, vegetable proteins and oils, cereals and in some cases herbs and shellfish.

If you feed fresh meat, you will need to feed a quality biscuit and perhaps some sort of supplement in the form of tablet or powder to provide the other elements that a dog requires. There are products which contain the carbohydrates, minerals, vitamins and herbs which are believed to constitute an accurate replica, apart from meat and fat, of the diet a dog would procure in the wild. But this is a bit of a juggling act and I prefer to use the dry complete foods, ringing the changes every so often as time goes by.

At seven weeks, puppies need to be fed quite frequently, say, four or even five times a day. This is because they need quite a lot of food and can assimilate it best in small regular amounts. People ask me how big each meal should be. I find it difficult to be exact – I look at a puppy and try to gauge what a tummyful would be. The manufacturers of the complete foods usually print on the bag the amounts that they recommend you feed, but generally speaking these are too big, and your puppy will become too fat. As a guide, I would say that you should feed less than you think, but if the puppy looks unrounded after his meals, or seems discontented with the amount, or begins to show too many ribs, you can gradually increase the size of each meal.

Some people advocate ad lib feeding, that is, having food available at all times, but I do not agree with this practice. Not only is this not natural for a dog, but it means that puppies will not have the frequent human contact that will attract them to their handler and help to foster a good relationship between owner and pup. Each time I take food to them, I call out, 'Come!' and blow the recall whistle. This really gives them a good start for one of the most important commands. After feeding, or after the 'bucket run', I try to spend a few minutes a couple of times a day just sitting with my puppies, playing with them, stroking them and generally getting them used to being handled. I might cut their toenails, inspect their ears, teeth, feet and coats. I lay them on my lap on their back and make a gentle fuss of them until they relax. All this prepares them for when they may have to visit the veterinarian for routine or special attention.

From early on, it is a good idea to accustom the youngster to sudden loud noises. The idea is to prepare him for the sound of gunfire. Start gradually with a not-too-loud noise such as a blown-up paper bag popped fairly gently just before you put his food bowl down for him. If he seems alarmed or fazed, get someone else to make the noise in the next room, after which you should praise him and put the food down. The noise must come before the food; if you do it the other way round, the dog will think he is being punished for eating. A large book slammed shut is another good way of making the right sort of noise. As time goes on, increase the loudness and proximity of the noise, being careful to introduce each new kind of noise at a fair distance or in another room, and gradually bringing it closer.

Another good use of mealtime is to teach the puppy to sit before he is given his food. Gradually you can build up his steadiness by making him wait in the sitting position while you put the bowl down, and then

Puppy looking up at the handler's face, waiting for permission to eat.

for longer and longer before you say 'Paid for', or your chosen command meaning he may eat. He must look up at you before you give him your command and signal meaning that he may eat: 'Sit' should mean 'Sit and look at me.'

I feel that the intake of water is an extremely important factor in the growth of young animals, and one good way of getting it into them is to feed them their food wetted. Fresh drinking water should always be available as well. When puppies are really small, I make sure the water bowl is shallow enough that they can get out of it if they should get into it. By the same token, I never leave buckets of water where they can climb into them. A puppy might be able to get into a bucket but not out – puppies have been known to drown in this way.

Of course, as a puppy grows, you will need to increase the amounts of food that you give, and by the eleventh or twelfth week you can begin to reduce the number of feeds to three per day. Do this by making the second meal gradually later and later until it is given at about four or five in the afternoon. Then the third meal can take the place of the fourth. Gradually, the last meal can be reduced to a few small dry biscuits at bedtime.

By the time the dog reaches six months, you should have reduced the number of meals to two a day, morning and evening. I feed a small breakfast to my dogs for the whole of their life, although it is a very small one on a working day. Feeding a dog a large meal before exercise can result in stomach torsion, which is a life-threatening condition.

The Middle Years

All brands of dog food claim to be the best that you ever put in your dog's mouth, but they are all slightly different. Over time, sticking with only one food, even though it seems to suit your dog, may create a problem. No one food can be right for all dogs, as all dogs are different, and the nutritional requirements of any dog will alter at different stages in his life. Thus the food you have been feeding happily for years may lack some minute ingredient that your particular dog needs, though it might take some considerable time for a defi-

ciency to be appreciated. My feed shed looks like an Aladdin's cave for dogs. Having a number of dogs, I will use up food quite quickly, so I can have several different foods on the go at any given time. I will feed perhaps seven or eight different brands and grades mixed together so as to provide a broader spectrum of nourishment than that obtained from just one. This method also accustoms a dog to variety so he is not affected by a sudden change in diet as he might be if he had to go to stay with someone else or at the vet's and his usual food was not available. Please note, however, that this technique is not suitable for young puppies, as it could lead to digestive upset.

Nor is it practical for someone with only one or two dogs to keep seven or eight bags of food open at once. What you could do, however, is to feed one or two types of food and then, after six months or a year, gradually introduce another food and simultaneously ease out one of the others.

My dogs have their main meal in the evening, which fits in well during the shooting season as they should not go to work on a full stomach. I feed a mix of good, middle-grade complete foods, wetted with warm water. In the shooting season I will usually add about three or four ounces of minced raw tripe. No one seems to know why tripe is so good for dogs, but it is the best thing I know for keeping condition on hard-working dogs. Minced tripe can usually be bought in frozen free-flow packs so that you can thaw what you need as you need it.

If I am away from home for the evening at the end of a shoot day, I will have food ready in the car and warm water in a flask to mix with it, and feed it about an hour after the finish of work.

Sadly, the sight of obese dogs is becoming more common these days. Not only is it expensive to make a dog overweight, but it is as bad for him as it would be for his handler. It puts a strain on every part of the body when you work a dog in this condition, and it is not a pretty sight. It can restrict a dog's abilities with regard to activities such as jumping, swimming and prolonged hunting, and will cause him to tire prematurely. A fit dog will show one or two of his back ribs, and it should be easy for you to feel the pin bones on either side of the root of the tail.

The condition of a dog's droppings is a good guide as to how a food is suiting him: they should be firm and sausage-shaped. It is sometimes quite surprising to see the disparate effects in colour and consistency that different dogs' digestive processes can have on the droppings, even though you may be feeding the same food to several different dogs. The variation in colour of normal droppings is quite broad. Normal colour can be from tan to very dark brown. Black can indicate the consumption of blood (bloody meat) or of the droppings of herbivores; it can also indicate bleeding in the stomach and upper part of the intestine, so be observant, and if it continues for more than a day or becomes red, consult your veterinary surgeon.

Bones can be a matter of contention. It cannot be denied that in nature, bones form part of a dog's normal diet and help to keep his teeth clean. But no one can know how many wild dogs die of internal injury or compaction in the gut from consuming bones. In domestication, it is generally accepted that the only bones one can safely give dogs are the raw bones of young chickens and other immature animals, or the whole marrow bones of large herbivores. A dog's jaws are amazingly powerful and I have found 2in-long pointed shards of marrow bones in a dog's droppings. How no injury was caused is a mystery.

Nowadays there are many products on the market which claim to help keep a dog's teeth clean and healthy, but they are expensive and have varying levels of benefit.

The Older Dog

All dogs are different, and, like us, they change with the passing years. They seem to have a short youth with a great deal of growth and change packed into it, a long middle life, and a relatively short old age. As dogs go into old age, their ability to chew and assimilate certain foods can alter. Amounts of food may need to be reduced and given at more frequent intervals, much as in puppyhood. Some dogs will develop tooth trouble, and their food should be made up of small bits softened by adding or soaking with warm water. However, these dogs should also be given a marrow bone to help remove tartar, sometimes called calculus, from their teeth. Occasionally a serious build-up of tartar will need to be removed by a veterinary surgeon under general anaesthetic. If your dog has to undergo surgery for some other reason, it would be well to note if the teeth need attention at the same time. A general anaesthetic always carries a risk, so frequent anaesthesia should be avoided.

If you notice that your dog has any particular food intolerances, or if he loses condition and does not seem to benefit from the food he eats, it will be worth consulting your veterinary surgeon who can recommend an appropriate diet or supplement for the dog. The dog may possibly need medication, such as in a case of heart trouble or diabetes.

THE OTHER END

Feeding is a very important aspect of dog management, but so too is dealing with the unavoidable result. Puppies can do eight or more poos a day, and adult dogs will do two or three.

These need to be cleaned up. In public places, it is the law that owners should clean up after their dogs. There are several reasons for this: although it is not common, certain canine worms can cause blindness in humans. Dog poo is extremely nasty to step in and very unpleasant if it gets in the tread of your car or mower tyres. Nowadays, hardly any dog owner goes away from home without a supply of poo bags in his or her pocket. They dutifully pick up their dog's droppings – but then what do they do with the offensive little sack? One often sees them festooning a fence or hedge. How revolting! If you pick up a dog's poo with a bag, please, please keep it with you and dispose of it at home, or find a bin to put it in.

At home, around the kennel and garden, for this most disliked job of clearing up poos, I use a coal shovel and a hoe with the handle shortened to about two feet. I take an old galvanized 10-litre bucket, no longer of use for water as it has a leak, and line it with grass cuttings, dead leaves or the like before I begin to fill it with the droppings. When I'm ready to empty the bucket, I cover the droppings with more grass or other non-stick biodegradable material, and empty the bucket on to an out-of-the-way heap. I expect the heap to look like a mound of garden waste, which is not unsightly and also keeps the flies at bay, and the plant material helps to compost the manure, although very, very slowly. Sometimes, in a good summer, it all dries out enough for me to set light to it, and once I had a heap that burned for sixteen days! After some years the heap goes down to an innocuous, non-odorous compost, which you may want to move to another place. I wouldn't want to sell it in bags at the gate or put it on my garden, but it can make a grassy bank or sound barrier.

Some dogs will eat their own faeces or those of other dogs, so clearing up should minimize this. This habit is revolting, but in some cases may be associated with feeding a poor quality diet – the ingredients passed resemble the ingredients in the dog's feed bowl. Sometimes this disgusting habit ceases as the dog reaches adulthood, though occasionally a dog will continue it throughout his life. I do not know a cure. I have tried muzzling the offending animals, but they will even try to eat messes through the muzzle! I have tried changing the dog's diet, adding supplements, adding ketchup, barbeque sauce, pineapple – almost anything the old wives have suggested – but nothing seems to work. Scolding doesn't work; the dog watches you and when he sees you are not looking he will get down to his beastly trick. It seems more common in bitches. Bitches are programmed to clear up their puppies' droppings. This would stem from the need to keep the den clean in the wild situation. As the puppies are weaned from their mother's milk on to solid food, most bitches gradually give up this unsavoury practice – but some do not. Other species also clean up after their young, but the dog is the only one I know which will persistently eat its own and other dogs' droppings. I believe this behaviour to be hereditary, although boredom may play a part in the case of some dogs.

ACCOMMODATION

Indoors and/or Outdoors?

Some people believe that a dog should live outdoors at all times, and that somehow this is beneficial to his training. I suppose that if the dog is alone in a kennel most of the time, he will be really keen when he comes out with you. But keen to do what? Race about certainly, but the dog that lives indoors is just as keen to go out with his owner. You will have to decide on this matter yourself. I have kept dogs in kennels and in the house, and a mixture of the two. I feel that all ways have their merits, but keeping a dog indoors teaches him that he is not the centre of the universe, that sometimes you are speaking to him and sometimes to someone else. He learns to relax in your presence.

His accommodation, wherever it is, should be dry and free from draughts, not necessarily heated, but snug, with some kind of bedding he can burrow into. Dogs do not tend to cuddle up to each other in kennels. This puzzles me, but whenever I have two or three dogs sharing the same bed box, I find two or three separate nests in the bedding, however cold the weather. Choice of bedding can be a teaser, but I have found that torn-up newspaper is the least of all evils. Newspaper tears easily one way and not the other. The best are the broadsheets as they take less time to tear. This job is restful and often informative, but I am careful not to give the dogs anything to read which extols the virtues of politicians I do not like! I sometimes get caught up in doing the crossword, but the dogs like having my company.

A run of a minimum of 4 × 6ft is a good idea to have attached to the bed box so that if you have to leave the dog for longer than he can 'hang on', he can use the run to spend his pennies. I find that a bigger run is seldom used for exercise; once a dog is adult, he sleeps most of the day and moves about his quarters very little. His main excitement would be to hear you coming or to bark at an intruder. Puppies do enjoy a big run, and using grass for their ablutions helps to teach them to be clean indoors.

EXERCISE

Some of the gundog breeds, particularly Labradors, are prone to the conditions known as hip dysplasia and elbow dysplasia. Both can cause lameness and arthritis in later life. Heredity plays a part in the development of these conditions, but much can be done by the owner to prevent them occurring or worsening. Puppies should be discouraged from standing on

ABOVE: *Puppy of four months being lifted into the car.*

BELOW: *Puppy of four months being helped down from the car.*

their hind legs or pulling on the lead. They should be lifted or helped into and out of cars, over fences and up steep steps, anywhere where the joints will be put under stress. When puppies play with older dogs they should be supervised, and sport should not be allowed to go on for more than a few minutes, less if the games are rough.

Careful feeding will ensure that the dog grows well but does not become overweight. Labrador puppies should not be taken for proper walks until they are about ten to twelve months of age. They can be given adequate physical exercise in several short outings a day, the duration of which should be about ten minutes each. The first can take place first thing in the morning before breakfast, another after breakfast, one at midday, one mid-afternoon, one after supper and one last thing before bed.

In the evenings you will find that your puppy becomes extra skittish and playful. This is a well known phenomenon in young lambs, which will gang together at about 7 o'clock in the early summer evenings and gambol about in a very lively way. If a puppy does not have a sibling or other dog to play with, I make up games for him to play with me. A good one for indoors is to show him out of the room – I say, 'Hide eyes', while I am sending him out – and then hide a tennis ball or screwed up piece of paper somewhere, perhaps under a chair or behind the door. He is then called into the room with the words, 'Hie lost'. When he is near the article I say 'Steady', and when he leaves the area I say, softly, 'No'. It's like the game we used to play as children, where the one who knew where the 'prize' was would say, 'You're getting warmer, warmer, boiling hot, no, cold now, colder, freezing…' This comes into his training again later. When he has played this game four or five times, he will usually settle down for a rest.

While a dog is in training with me, his exercise is still restricted to the six short outings per day, with part of one of them just for training. The training part does not last long – I have found that six minutes is optimum. Short, accompanied outings keep the dog focused on me. I am the one who opens the door, so to the dog, I must be a bit special. A long walk where the dog may be out of sight of his handler for a period of time encourages independence – not a good thing when you are trying to develop a sort of team spirit between the two of you. It also fills the dog's nose with exciting smells, his eyes and ears with exciting sights and sounds, and hence his mind with ideas which are not related to training. Training is, after all, mostly curbing or channelling instinct. To allow the development of independence is to risk the dog learning that chasing is fun and coming to or being with you is not fun.

When you have completed the basic training, and you know your dog is reliable on the stop whistle and will come instantly when called, you will be able to allow the dog more freedom, knowing that he is under control. Be honest with yourself over this, and do not allow him free rein until you are truly confident in his obedience. It sounds mean, but if you think about it, it is not as mean as corrective training.

When a dog is coming into full work, exercise must be gradually increased in order to get him fit. A shooting day can be gruelling. On the day after shooting, exercise can be light, but on subsequent days you should give him enough exercise to make him pant. (Perhaps the same should be said of the handler!) You must not allow your dog to lose condition. He should maintain a high level of fitness throughout the shooting season, though perhaps he may be let off a little once it is over. However, if you are keen on competing, you may wish to run him in tests during the summer, in which case he needs to be kept fit for these, too.

As your dog passes into old age he needs to be kept in good condition, but when you notice that he is slowing down or has perhaps developed some joint problem, you should begin to reduce the distance you take him. The bursts of speed that he formerly enjoyed may exhaust him more readily, and you must take care to pace him, as probably he will not pace himself. The amount of jumping he does should be restricted, and he should be helped over or guided around high obstacles. The effort needed to get over a jump is one aspect, but it is just as important to consider the impact of landing, because it could have a harmful effect on his joints.

GROOMING

The Labrador's coat needs little grooming, though some

Biscuit at ten years of age. A great game-finder and my 'right-hand man' for many years – mostly self-employed – I was just the chauffeur!

may need a brush through when they are moulting. If you have two or more dogs that are friends with each other, they will groom each other in play and when lying together – the coat gets a lot of beneficial attention from the jostling, play-biting and ragging they give each other. A brush with wire bristles on one side of the head and normal, fairly firm bristles on the other is a good one to have. This and a couple of metal combs – one with closely spaced teeth and the other with widely spaced teeth – will probably be all you will ever use. You should always check for thorns and brambles after an outing in dense cover.

Ears, on the other hand, seem to need regular and frequent attention. Because Labradors are 'flop-eared',

air cannot circulate in the ear canal as it can in the case of prick-eared dogs. This enables mites to thrive and ear wax to build up, which can easily lead to irritation and infection. The ear wax in dogs is dark, almost black in colour, which can make you think that things are worse than they are. However, the wax does accumulate, and you should clear out the worst of it on a regular basis.

The ear canal of the dog goes down alongside the head and turns a right angle before it reaches the eardrum. You can feel the cartilaginous funnel from the outside if you run your finger and thumb down from the open cup of the ear. For this reason, when you are cleaning the ear, you can probe with a cotton bud a

Cross-section of canine ear canal.

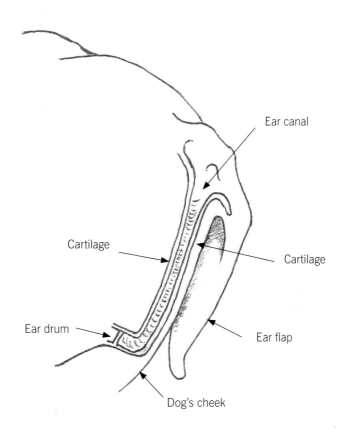

Ear canal

Cartilage

Cartilage

Ear drum

Ear flap

Dog's cheek

good way down without fear of damaging the eardrum. However, you should always be extremely gentle – you must not cause damage to the ear canal, and you must certainly not cause pain, as the dog will not allow you to treat his ears again without a tussle. I twist extra cotton wool around the tip of the cotton bud to make it fatter, which makes it more comfortable and more effective – though you must always be certain that you have not left any cotton wool in the ear canal. Use a cotton-wool swab to clean the outer ear. You can obtain very good ear-cleaning fluids from your veterinary surgeon, which soften and dislodge the wax, and also products that kill ear mites. Be sure to follow the instructions.

The toenails of an active dog, especially one which is kept in a kennel with a concrete run, will seldom need attention. A dog which lives indoors will occasionally need his claws cut back. A dog's claws are very tough and there are special clippers available for dealing with them, but great care must be taken: only cut off a little at a time, because if you cut the quick it is extremely painful and the dog may never let you touch his feet again! Some breeders remove the dewclaws shortly after birth, but this is not often done with Labradors; I have seldom found that they cause problems, and in fact, some people say dewclaws help a dog to climb over stone walls. The nail does not often come into contact with any surface which will wear it down, so check the dewclaws from time to time and clip them back carefully.

Young dogs should become accustomed to being handled and groomed from an early age; this will pay dividends should you ever have to take your dog to the vet. Be gentle but firm; the muzzle-holding technique can be helpful here – *see* Chapter 4.

DEALING WITH PARASITES

Endoparasites (Worms)

Throughout his life, your dog will be picking up worm eggs from the soil and his surroundings. It is unavoidable, and certain worm eggs can survive for many years in the right conditions. Some worms in small quantities can be tolerated by a dog without ill effect, but I resent feeding worms when it is already costly enough to feed the dog! A heavy worm burden can be debilitating for a dog, and I have found that it can affect behaviour and trainability.

As a result of climate change, there is an increase in the incidence of lungworm – a potentially lethal parasite – in the south of England. It occurs in dogs through the eating of slugs and snails, or licking where their trails lie. Treat your dog regularly, using a medicine from your veterinary surgeon. Some of those sold in a pet shop have to be so safe, in case a child should take them off the shelf, that they are just not effective. There are some effective products sold in pet shops and over the Internet, but would you contact the vendors when you have an emergency? I think it is only fair to give your veterinarian the business, besides which he can keep you informed of any new developments in the fight against endoparasites.

Puppies need to be treated more frequently than adults, ideally monthly for the first six months.

There are now products that will act against both endo- and ectoparasites, including ear mites. Consult your veterinary surgeon.

Ectoparasites

Ectoparasites include all the parasites that live in or on the skin. The most common in the domestic dog are fleas, ticks, lice, ear mites, sarcoptic and demodectic mange, ringworm and Cheyletiella. They are acquired by contact with infected animals, bedding or carpets, or grass where infected animals have lain or brushed through.

Fleas are very persistent in that their pupae can lie dormant for long periods, hatching spontaneously when a living animal passes by, causing vibrations in the surroundings. So it can be seen that in the case of fleas, the dog and its living quarters need to be treated at the same time. Most modern products for use on the dog or its environment last for longer than the life cycle of the flea, therefore more than one pupal hatch. Take advice from your veterinarian and read the product directions carefully. Tapeworms and fleas are closely associated, so treatment for both should take place simultaneously.

Mange and ringworm are very tricky, and your veterinary surgeon is the one to supply help and advice. If you suspect either of these problems, do not be slow in taking your dog to the surgery. Ringworm is transmissible to humans, and mange is very contagious between dogs, and will cause them considerable misery.

Cheyletiella is a tiny mite, not visible to the naked eye. It seems to cause much more irritation in puppies than in adults. It thrives in the skin and makes a sensitive host scratch constantly. It can be very distressing to small puppies. It appears as a kind of dandruff on the coat, and can make the skin furrowed and creased like that of a rhinoceros. I have found that the spray-on insecticides are effective where the 'spot-on' ones are not. Two treatments about ten days apart seems to work best. The mite does not appear to live off the animal, being passed from one dog to another.

INOCULATIONS

Inoculation against the more serious canine diseases is a matter for you to arrange with your veterinary surgeon. Through inoculation, serious canine diseases such as distemper, leptospirosis, hepatitis and parvovirus are seldom seen nowadays, but they are extremely distressing illnesses, often with a fatal conclusion. There are currently some people who propose that inoculations are not necessary or even good for dogs, but I would wager that these are people who have never seen a case of, for example, distemper. I have, and I sincerely hope never to see it again.

When you enter a competition held under Kennel Club rules, you must sign a declaration stating that your dog has been inoculated against the usual canine diseases. There is good reason for this rule, and it really is important to keep your dog's inoculations up to date because he is bound to go out in public from time to time and will occasionally be exposed to infection.

Kennel cough is a particularly contagious and virulent infection. While seldom causing death, it is very debilitating, and using an affected dog for work could put a serious strain on the heart. I have found that it is the dog that is in his prime that suffers the most with 'the cough'; puppies and old dogs seem to shake it off more easily. There is a good prophylactic vaccine commonly referred to as the 'sniff vaccine', which is administered by a veterinary surgeon. It is introduced intra-nasally and can protect a dog for up to a year from kennel cough. Kennel cough is very contagious, so if you hear of an outbreak, keep away from the source if you can. Similarly, if your dog contracts it, be considerate and keep him quarantined for at least ten days after he has stopped coughing.

As with worming products, vaccinations can be purchased privately and through the Internet, but the substances used must be kept at stable, set temperatures and there is a chance that these will not be maintained during transit. The network used by your veterinary surgeon and his facilities at the surgery are designed to sustain the correct conditions. Included in the price of inoculation, your veterinarian will give your dog a thorough check-up. Inoculations will not 'take' if a dog is already fighting an infection, and your vet will be able to tell from his temperature and the state of his glands whether he is well enough to be inoculated. I would not risk my dog's life, not to mention my peace of mind, for the sake of saving a few pounds.

AILMENTS

I do not intend to go into this subject very deeply, but I will say that if you know your dog well, you will know when he is 'off colour'. You should take note of any unusual behaviour, or a change in timing of his bodily functions.

Taking his temperature is one of the best ways of finding out if you should be concerned enough to enlist the help of your veterinary surgeon. You should take the dog's temperature before you ring the vet so that you can tell him what it is when you reach him. Normal is around 101.2°F or between 37.5 and 38.8°C, and the temperature should be taken rectally with a rectal thermometer. Check that the mercury is right down, or that the reading is at zero. The dog's rectum follows a parallel line, approximately, to the line of the spine as it leads into the body. You may need an assistant to hold the dog still, and the thermometer should be kept about an inch inside him for at least 30 seconds. Clean the thermometer with cotton wool which you have wetted with alcohol or some antiseptic. After you have read the temperature, make sure you shake down the mercury, or next time you may be reading the old temperature. The modern thermometers work in a different way and do not need to be shaken down – just follow the instructions.

You can tell a great deal about a dog's condition from the state of his droppings. The normal consistency of droppings is firm and sausage-shaped, not like porridge or soup. A covering of a jelly-like substance can be a forewarning of infection or a sign of worms. The odour of dog droppings is repellent to humans (and, strangely, it seems that dog faeces smell worse when they have been trodden in!) but the smell should not be exceptionally foul.

There are many causes of 'runny tummy', including eating too much, eating things that have 'gone off', and infection. If a dog develops diarrhoea but otherwise seems jolly, I would suspect that he has eaten something he should not have. He should be starved for twelve hours and then fed small quantities of a bland diet: semolina, pasta, cooked chicken and rice, or scrambled egg would be suitable choices. Rice that has been kept warm for more than an hour is not safe. Fluids are very important, so I usually make any mixture fairly wet and add a small amount of salt and honey to make it more palatable. A spoonful of cat food seems to raise interest in dull food, too. If after two days the dog seems happy but his faeces continue to be abnormal, consult your veterinary surgeon. If the dog seems depressed and continuously refuses food, do not delay in seeking veterinary advice.

I have found that there is usually an outbreak of gastric disturbance in the kennel after we have had snow. This sort of diarrhoea usually needs veterinary attention.

Diarrhoea can have blood in it, which can be quite alarming. The trouble with blood is that it is so red, but while blood in the faeces should be taken as a serious sign, try to keep calm. It can indicate infection; it could also mean that the dog has ingested something sharp, such as a bone shard. Veterinary advice should be sought.

It can be normal for a dog to regurgitate his food or to vomit once a week. Persistent vomiting – that is, more than six times a day, or continuing for more than forty-eight hours – would indicate the need to consult a veterinary surgeon.

If your dog seems one degree under and there is nothing obvious, look at his gums and the inner rim of the eye. The colour should be a warm salmon pink, and not red, grey or white. If you press the gum so that it goes white, it should return to a good colour within a second or two of releasing the pressure. If the gum remains pale for longer, this is a cause for concern.

Always remember that common things occur commonly. Thus you will gradually learn to deal with the common ailments such as sickness and diarrhoea, and minor eye, ear and skin problems, and eventually you will come to recognize when the symptoms shown are those of a condition with which you are not qualified to deal. Veterinary attention is private medicine and can be expensive, but generally excellent care and treatment are given. Besides the affection you may have for him, your dog-in-training and the trained gundog are valuable, not just in terms of cost and the time you have spent on them, but for their usefulness in the field and possibly from a breeding point of view. Money spent on expert advice will seldom be a waste under these circumstances.

CHAPTER 4

HOW DOGS LEARN

A dog is a dog. Using selective breeding, humans may have altered dogs outwardly to look more like gazelles, or bears, or humans, but in their mind and instincts they are still dogs. Again, by selecting dogs of pack member type as opposed to pack leader type, temperament has been established which suits humans – a pack member type has a juvenile nature and is naturally submissive, which makes a dog easier to train and to keep on training. Our modern domestic dog – and I am thinking here particularly of our Labrador – is a tribute to the efforts of our forebears, and we have much to thank them for, but he is still a dog, not a human: he is a different species, and is still governed by pack instincts and behaviours. Be careful not to spell dog backwards.

Training is channelling a dog's instincts and abilities to our use. If you understand the way he views things and the way he learns, if you use his submissiveness properly, it is possible to make your dog into a very enjoyable and valuable sporting companion.

DOGS ARE PACK ANIMALS

In the wild, dogs live in groups we call packs. There are usually several pack members and two pack leaders, a dog and a bitch. The leaders decide everything. They choose where the pack goes, where it rests, when and what they will hunt. They always sleep in a higher physical position than the other dogs, eat first, and are in fact the only ones to breed – the other females in the pack tend not to come into season. Nature has a way of suppressing their season. The leaders' rule is absolute while they are fit and well, and they maintain it through swift and physical punishment of any dog that opposes them.

Puppies learn the boundaries at a very early age. Their mother will tolerate a certain amount of 'taking liberties' in play, but when she has had enough, she draws the line. If you watch a mother dog with puppies of around six weeks of age and upwards, you will see that when a puppy is particularly annoying, she will growl and cover his muzzle, and perhaps eyes, with her mouth. She is not biting the pup, just holding him still. She may place a forepaw on his neck or shoulder to help keep him from resisting. The pup becomes catatonic, quiet and submissive. She will hold him there for several seconds, growling all the while, and then will slowly let him go. Very often, the young offender will immediately leap up exuberantly and equally as annoyingly as before, and the whole performance will be repeated. If he persists, she may eventually give him a sharp nip which leaves him yelping and chastened, but not traumatized. This treatment teaches the pup that growling and muzzle-holding are a warning of something worse. It teaches him submissiveness, and when the male leader and other dogs growl at him, he will understand what he should do. He will adopt a submissive posture in order to be accepted and to avoid being bitten.

The father dog, the male leader of the pack, will use the warning growl with puppies, followed by a bite if he is ignored, but he tends to use a more severe punishment on adolescent and adult miscreants. He will seldom look at a pack member, but if he does, it is because he is very displeased. If this does not produce submissiveness in the subordinate dog, the leader will attack without hesitation, always from above, usually on the neck. This is where the expression 'top dog' originates. In cases where the pack member does not submit, the pack leader's aim will be to get the upstart on his back on the ground where he can give him a good trouncing. His object is to put the pack member 'in his place'. He does not want to harm the pack member – he needs his help and co-operation to ensure the smooth running of the whole pack system – but he must have absolute compliance, and he will not tolerate challenges to his leadership.

In the case of an outsider dog trying to invade the pack, the leader will brook no nonsense: he will attack, and other pack members will back him up. The interloper will nearly always show submission in the face of this concerted front. He understands that there is zero tolerance of insubordination, and if he wishes to join the pack he must submit to the leader's authority and take a place at an appropriate level in the pack.

Suffice it to say, therefore, that in order to impress your dog sufficiently for him to accept you as his pack leader, you must dominate him in a way he understands. This means that you will have to cause him some embarrassment or discomfort. As a rule of thumb, just consider that you are not likely to hurt or upset him more than he would be hurt or upset in play with another dog. After all, if you have seen dogs at play, you know that they can be really rough with each other – they make each other holler! The average person who is fond of his dog is seldom likely to do that.

Many people are afraid that they will 'damage the relationship' they have with their dog if they correct or punish it. This is not the case. Our Labrador is a pack member type, and as such he needs to know who his pack leader is. If the handler does not demonstrate, in a way that the dog understands, that he is the dominant one, the dog will cast about looking for his leader. Not finding one, he will assume that it is he himself – but because he does not have the right characteristics, he will make a poor job of it, and the handler will end up with a 'problem dog'.

Dominance in the handler does not mean brutality or violence. Brutality and violence are counter productive because they cause fear. A being cannot function fully in a fearful state – the ability to learn will be impaired, and what is remembered of a lesson may vary greatly to what was intended.

Submissive does not mean nervous. Submissiveness is innate. We have found that the more submis-sive a dog is, the more trainable he is. Most of our domesticated working breeds have been derived from submissive, pack member types.

If you as handler are to be 'top dog' – the leader – it is important to achieve dominance in your relationship with your dog, and to do this you must demonstrate your authority using body language. This includes carrying yourself in a positive way, maintaining an upright posture, keeping your chin up, not looking at the dog when he is excited, and not touching him below eye level.

The positive, upright posture simulates the proud, confident bearing of the pack leader. Keeping your chin up means you will not be glaring full face at the dog, which is perceived by him as threatening. Not looking at him demonstrates your aloofness and superiority. Touching him below eye level is perceived by a dog as submissive. Note that you can tickle or scratch a dog on the chest or tummy when he is on his back, because your hands will then still be above eye level, will be between him and the sky.

THE MUZZLE-HOLDING TECHNIQUE

In addition to using body language, you can use the muzzle-holding technique that the dog's mother taught him when he was a baby. This technique, modified, can be used by humans as a 'tool', which remains effective in the training of a dog for the whole of his life. The reason we would modify this, or any other canine behaviour, is chiefly from a hygiene point of view. We do not, usually, wish to lick or bite dogs! But we have hands which we can use *in lieu* just as effectively.

It is important at this point to explain just how this technique should be carried out. One hand should hold the dog by the collar or scruff at the back of the neck, and the other should be placed over the dog's face. Note in the drawing how the thumb is placed on one side of the muzzle and the fingers lie on the other. The pressure is firm, but in no way is it a grip or pinch. The technique is most effective if the eyes are partially or wholly covered. The hold should not hurt the dog, only chasten it. If the hold is being used in correcting the dog, the handler should grumble at the dog and rate him sternly but not loudly. If the dog shows signs of

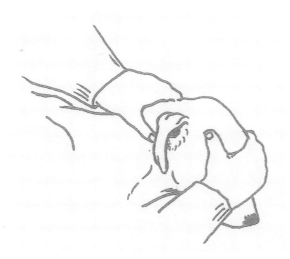

The muzzle-holding technique   The handler holds the dog by the scruff with one hand as firmly as is necessary to keep him still. With the other hand he covers the dog's muzzle, thumb on one side, fingers on the other, and applies a gentle downward pressure. This stimulates the treatment his mother applied when she wanted to 'put him in his place' as a puppy. It subdues a scatty dog, calms a nervous dog and makes a flighty dog concentrate. Covering the dog's eyes increases the benefit. The hold on the muzzle is never a grip but the handler may grip the scruff firmly. The hold should be applied for several seconds and should be released slowly for the technique to have full effect.

submission, he should be held for about seven seconds and then slowly released. The signs of submission include showing the whites of the eyes, panting and/or smiling, licking the lips, putting the ears back, lowering the tail, and feebly wagging the tail.

If the dog resists the hold, take a stronger grip on the collar or scruff and press downwards. This should be done firmly but not roughly. You may need to press certain very wilful dogs right down to the ground, still keeping the gentle hold on the muzzle. This type of dog may need to be held down for a minute or more, and you should be scolding in a firm but not loud voice all the while. Your aim is to gain acceptance, so you must resist any temptation to use violence. Violence tends to escalate, and will result in the dog being either aggressive or fearful in the future. Look for any signs of relaxation or submission, and as soon as you see them, start to speak in a kind voice, though still restraining

the dog. This is a landmark in your relationship, and it may mean a very important turning point, so manage it carefully. Take time over this and do not let him up

The muzzle-holding technique: the handler is keeping the young Labrador still with her left hand on his scruff, while her right hand covers his muzzle. There is a downward pressure in the right hand but no hint of a grip. This makes the dog subdued but not afraid. It is similar to the treatment he would have received as a puppy from his mother if she needed to 'put him in his place'.

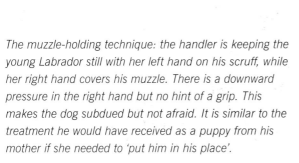

The muzzle-holding technique – the handler's right hand covers the dog's muzzle and partially obscures his vision. He is showing his submission by putting out the tip of his tongue, and by his posture.

You don't always have to sound cross when you use this technique: it is not just for use when the dog has done wrong. You can do it casually dozens of times a day, just because you can: it puts you in the driver's seat, it calms a nervous dog, and it concentrates the mind of a scatty dog. Be sure you always keep your hand over his muzzle for several seconds, and release him very slowly. Partially or completely covering the eyes can make this treatment doubly effective.

One of the best things about the muzzle-holding technique is that it is so well accepted by a dog: he

too soon. When you do release him, do so very slowly. As you release your hold, put the lead on, make friends with him, stroking him above eye level but with your face turned away from his.

The use of this technique teaches him the physical meaning of your cross voice, and when he hears it in the future, he will think that you may be about to apply the hold again, reminding him, physically, of your position of dominance. When his mother did it, he knew it was a warning of worse to come if he ignored it, so he will want to avoid getting into your bad books, and to avoid hearing the words 'bad dog'.

After applying the muzzle-holding technique, the handler should always be friendly but calm with the pupil. It can be seen that the youngster is calm, happy and accepting: he is subdued but not upset.

is not frightened by it – even when it is employed by a complete stranger – because it is something he encountered when he was very young, something he received from his dear and trusted mother. Even the grip on the collar or scruff is well accepted because it is something he learnt from his superiors when he was young, and because it does not hurt.

PRAISE AND REWARD

The best that a pack member in the wild can expect is to be ignored; he would not receive a kind word or a pat on the back from the leader for good or clever work.

We humans, on the other hand, are very different. We enjoy a compliment for a job well done, and we certainly like a reward. When we bring a dog into our lives, we do so partly because we like dogs: we like the way they feel, and we like the way they respond to kindness. A dog enjoys being fondled and stroked, lots of pats on his side, having his back and tummy scratched. When we couple these physical pleasures with kind words and praise, the dog learns the meaning of the kind voice. He revels in it, and strives to be the dog that merits the praise.

Your Labrador is your sporting companion, and the point of it all is for it to be fun. So I like to think that we are trying to find ways to make the training fun, trying to gain the dog's interest so that he wants to learn what we wish to impart. This in turn will improve his performance in each training session, and thus our mutual pleasure later in the field.

In my opinion, edible rewards do have a place in training. They should be small, and not take a lot of chewing before they are swallowed. They should be kept in one pocket, preferably the one on the opposite side to the one on which the dog walks to heel, as he should not be sniffing or pulling at your pocket all the time. They should be used sporadically, and randomly, and not every time the dog is asked to do something, nor every time he does a thing correctly. You don't want to reach a situation where the dog stands off from you and says, 'What have you got for me if I do what you say?'. I find a titbit very useful when teaching the sit and heelwork, but I do not use it in conjunction with the retrieve. The retrieve itself is the reward.

Dogs do not achieve their best in the working context purely out of their affection for us, nor will they perform well in the hope of praise, pats or edible reward. Respect for us is the key, and to gain this we need to employ methods that the dog understands. Of course he can learn to understand harsh punishments and respond to them, but the correction methods I use appeal to his nature and remind him of his mother's behaviour towards him when he was a small puppy.

Training a dog is most effectively achieved by using a balance of dominance displays and corrections on the one hand, together with praise and physical pleasure on the other. Although the best a pack member in the wild can expect is to be ignored, we know how much a dog enjoys a pat and a kind word, and it certainly accelerates his rate of learning if we balance correction with praise. Correction gives us one tool, and praise gives us another.

DOGS ONLY DO WHAT THEY FIND PREFERABLE

If a dog finds a certain action physically pleasurable or rewarding, he will tend to repeat it. For example, if he finds an egg and accidentally drops it, he will discover the contents smell good and gobble them up: he will learn that it is well worthwhile to repeat the exercise. Whereas if he finds that an action produces an unpleasant, uncomfortable or embarrassing result, he will tend to avoid it or refuse to repeat it. For example, if your dog puts his nose against a hot coffee cup, he will tend not to do it again: he discovers it is preferable not to do it.

Part of my method of training is to make what I want him to do a preferable experience. I do this by praising him – saying 'Good dog' and the like, fondling him, or sometimes rewarding him with a titbit when he does what I want. When I see an adverse response to a command, I scold him, saying such things as 'No!', 'Aaah!' and 'Bad dog!', and correcting him physically, frequently using the muzzle-holding technique. The dog is therefore either 'good' or 'bad', comfortable or uncomfortable: it's an 'either/or' world, and he soon realizes that he wants to be the 'good dog' and avoid being the 'bad dog'.

In the wild pack, life is very much black and white with practically no grey areas, and having studied many successful trainers, I notice that their approach is also very black and white. They are the ones who achieve the best results, and those of us who are 'grey' do not.

A DOG'S RESPONSES ARE IMMEDIATE

We would all like to do what is preferable, but we humans have a sense of the future. We know that if we don't wash the dishes now, we won't have anything clean to eat off later. Dogs are more immediate, in that what happens now is what matters to them. So if a dog is pottering along and a bird or a rabbit jumps up from under his nose, he doesn't look at his watch and say, 'Well, it's only ten past and as a rule I don't actually chase anything until a quarter past': on the contrary, he's off! His response is immediate. It follows, therefore, that his response to any stimulus, or indeed our commands, could also be immediate. By the same token, our responses to his behaviour should be quick. In order to impress a dog, it behoves us to be 'Swift to chide and swift to bless' (to alter the line of a well known hymn).

Timing in dog training, as with all aspects of life, is crucial if you are to have success. The time to praise is at the exact moment that you see the response you wish to see, and the time to scold is at the exact moment that you see something you do not wish to see. This takes a high degree of concentration, and you must work at getting it right until acting at the correct time becomes second nature.

DOGS LEARN BY PHYSICAL ASSOCIATION

Training a dog includes teaching him the meaning of a number of human sounds and words. Like a baby, he is born unable to understand even the language of his own kind. He only learns the meaning of language through the consequences of his actions – or non-action – in response to the sounds he hears, and what he sees, smells, feels or tastes. For example, he pulls his mother's ear, she growls, he ignores her because

he doesn't know the meaning of the sound, she nips him, he learns. This is called learning by association.

It is often said that dogs learn by association, but it should be emphasized that it should be physical association. When we bring a dog into our life, we do so for a number of reasons. One is that we like the feel of a dog's coat and we like to see the pleasure he shows when we pat and fondle him. While we are doing this, we tell the dog how good and clever he is. He doesn't have to do anything very wonderful for us to treat him like this. But do we realize that we are teaching the dog something? We are teaching him the physical meaning of our pleasant tone of voice when it is applied to him. This then becomes a 'tool' with which we convey to a dog that he is doing the 'right' thing.

Equally, we need a 'tool' associated with our cross tone of voice to tell him that he is out of favour, a demonstration of our displeasure, a correction. The sort of correction that a dog understands best is the one he learnt from his mother – the muzzle-holding technique described previously. This technique can be used by humans as a 'tool', which remains effective in the training and handling of a dog for the whole of his life. Interestingly, however, this technique is ineffective in a young pup until the handler has 'nipped' him – pinched him – as his mother eventually would have.

As mentioned above, this technique has three basic effects: it puts the handler in a position of authority – he becomes a pack leader. It calms an apprehensive dog because it puts the handler in the driver's seat, meaning that the dog can hand over responsibility for his safety to his handler. It makes a dog that is not concentrating focus on his handler. You can use this technique liberally without it losing effectiveness.

A DOG'S PERCEPTION OF MOVEMENT

It is extraordinary to me that what a dog sees is more important to them than what he hears. that is because they are very short-sighted. If, for instance, you dress in different clothes and wear a funny hat and stand or walk in an unusual way, your dog may well bark at you quite fiercely. Their perception of movement, however, is extremely acute. They will see a squirrel run up a tree at a huge distance! It is very helpful, therefore, to have hand signals to go with our commands. In fact, once a command is learnt with a signal, the latter will usually suffice when the dog is looking at you. The signal should have a degree of movement in it so that the dog can make it out. For example, the signal for 'Sit' will be the flat hand raised level with and to one side of your head. The action of raising your hand is part of the signal. If more movement is required, a small pushing motion of the hand will suffice.

It is very important that all your signals are clear and distinct from one another. For example, the raised hand for the 'Sit' should be no higher than your forehead because the signal for 'Get on' ('Go further away from me') is a hand raised above your head, and so will be quite different. Indeed, for 'Get on', I raise my hand to the height of my chin, then give an emphatic flick straight upwards as high as I can reach. This makes it very distinct from the 'Sit' signal. There is a movement of around three feet in this signal for 'Get on'. Even at a distance, the 'Sit' signal should stay level with your face and so will appear to the dog as two blobs side by side.

DOGS LEARN IN PICTURES

The concept of dogs 'learning in pictures' follows on from the previous point. When a dog learns something, he associates it with the place in which he learnt it, and the objects and other beings which were in that place. For example, I once lived near a dairy farm where I was allowed to walk my dogs. Single strand mains electric fencing was used to contain the cattle. Each of my dogs eventually touched the fencing with their tails and received a shock. They believed that (a) I had caused it, and (b) they were not safe in open country in that area, and they would not leave me, even when enthusiastically encouraged, until we came to woodland. Then they would happily gallop off and not give me the dirty looks I got on the farm.

Many people tell me that their dog behaves beautifully at home but is naughty elsewhere. This is because when you change the setting, the dog believes everything is changed. If your dog grasps the meaning of a command in a particular place, he will not necessarily respond to the command in another place. In effect he is saying, 'I never heard that word here so it cannot mean the same thing.' You will find that you will need to reteach the command in a variety of places, with a variety of different objects and other people and animals present, before he becomes reliable on that command. It becomes easier as you go on until eventually the penny drops. Then the dog seems to say, for example, 'Oh, sit means sit everywhere, whatever the circumstances.'

A fellow trainer says, 'Twenty different places with twenty different other dogs and twenty different people before you can say the dog has definitely learnt the command.'

THE PHYSIOLOGY OF LEARNING

Dogs need time for lessons to gel. Research has shown that physical activity or any use of the senses, such as occurs in a training session, triggers electrical activity among the brain cells. The electrical activity causes certain proteins present in the brain to move about and assist in the building of connections in the synapses (the gaps between the brain cells), and what might be called 'pathways' are created. With repetition, these pathways become marked, and form the long-term memory of the skills which have been learned. These pathways take time – some believe about twenty-four to forty-eight hours – to form, and are improved by repetition of the lesson. Their successful formation is aided by quiet rest after the activity.

It can easily be seen, then, how important it is that what your dog learns is what you want him to learn. It is just as easy for a dog (or any of us) to learn 'bad' things as it is for him to learn 'good' ones. With repetition, things become habit and we know how hard it is to break a habit! So I repeat: make sure that what you are teaching is what you want the dog to learn. Equally, it is obvious that once you see the glimmer of understanding, you repeat the exercise to get it to set. Remember the two R's: Repetition of what you really want the dog to learn, and Rest afterwards. These are vital keys to successful training.

Our chief aim with our Labrador is to achieve perfect retrieving, and it is really important that we do all we can to nurture this and avoid causing problems. You must try your best to help build the right pathways in the dog's brain.

It is interesting to note that if a dog has a particularly intense learning experience, whether good or bad, the memory which is formed from just that one experience is very strong. If the incident was particularly frightening, for instance, you may never get the dog over it. On the other hand, if it was particularly pleasurable for the dog, the memory which is formed will be lasting. Usually the pleasurable sort of incident involved is something we would deem to be undesirable, such as running-in, and sadly if a dog has 'got away with it' even just once, it can become a set habit which makes his steadiness unreliable for ever. This is what we would call a bad memory, a bad habit.

To a dog, all things he carries in his mouth basically

Two-year-old Labrador at heel looking up at his handler who is looking down at him. They are focused on each other.

represent food. Even the toys he plays with, tears and chews are food substitutes – he is practising dealing with quarry he has hunted down and needs to kill. The retrieve is ultimately food, and the retrieving instinct is based on the dog's innate wish: his need to bring food back to the lair for the puppies or the lead bitch when she is lactating.

Because this is the case, you must be careful not to scold a dog for having the 'wrong' things in his mouth. This might be shoes, clothing, the children's toys, carrion, cow pats, even the Sunday joint! You cannot expect him to differentiate between your precious silk stockings and his own juicy bone, because to him, it is either food or a food substitute. On seeing the precious or revolting article in the dog's mouth, you may have the urge to explode at the dog and order him to spit it out. What long-lasting repercussions this may have! When young, a dog cannot be expected to understand your view on every different item. Later when he understands the set of circumstances that surround the retrieve, you will be able to teach him to leave certain things and bring others.

You must not bore your dog. When you see that he has grasped a principle, praise and/or reward him, and put him away. If, after a training session, you put the dog away alone in a quiet place with the minimum of stimuli present – no toys, no food – the lesson will have time to gel: I find that ten to sixty minutes, by himself, is good. In your next session you will find that he has remembered the previous lesson and you can build on it.

Sometimes you will find that your dog does not understand what it is that you are trying to teach him, and this often shows in an expression that we perceive as one of defiance. It is not defiance, however: it is lack of understanding, and you will have to think of another way to put your message across, and the sooner the better. What must be avoided at all costs is the dog learning to do an exercise badly or sloppily because you have let him think that that is the way to do it. The wrong memory pathway will start to be formed, and if you repeat it, the pathway will become more and more concrete.

It is equally important that you do not become irritated by his lack of understanding, because you could make him fearful, and he cannot function well when he is afraid. You must try to think of another way to teach what you wish to impart. It is our job to get on to his 'wavelength', and to understand how he thinks, not the other way around.

Another sign that a dog does not understand what you want is that he looks at you and gives a sharp bark. The remedy is the same – find another way.

The best plan to follow when going out for a training session is to exercise the dog first, which should include some free running to let off steam. Then have your training session, the content of which you have thought out beforehand. After the lesson, which must end on a good note, put him on the lead and return him to his quiet place. This can be the car or kennel, and he should remain alone for at least ten minutes. In this way, the last things that you did are the things the dog remembers. If you train first, then allow free running, the dog will fill his nose with scent and his head with excitement, and the lesson will be pushed aside. Time spent alone after this will not then have much value.

CHAPTER 5

SOCIAL GRACES

A good gundog must have certain social niceties in order to complete his education. He should be quiet and polite in the house, car and kennel. He should not guard game either on the ground or in a vehicle. Some dogs guard the vehicle to the extent that other dogs and even people are afraid to enter. This is not acceptable.

He must not jump up against cars. He must not jump up against people or lick their hands or sniff them in inappropriate places!

A cage is a wonderful thing. In the car, it keeps a dog from destroying his surroundings so you know you need never be cross with him when you come back

A good sort of car cage. The dog has plenty of room to move around, but limited viewing available. This can help prevent car sickness and is good when the dog must be in his quiet place to 'think things over'. The bar-shaped gadget hanging from the front gate is a Ventlock, which is used to allow the tailgate to be locked but kept open a few centimetres for ventilation. (Courtesy Ventlock.com)

to him. It prevents him from stealing the groceries or shaking water, or worse, all over the interior of the car. It keeps him confined and therefore relatively still in the vehicle which, apart from stopping him from distracting the driver, helps prevent car sickness. Naturally, you need to accustom him to the cage gradually (see Chapter 2), but if you make it nice for him, he will look forward to being in it. He can have his toys and a bone in the cage, he can be fed his meals in it, and he will soon learn that he goes to nice places in it.

A cage will obviously be useful in the house, too, if your dog is to live indoors. It will become his own personal space where he can rest or chew his bone in peace. When you have non-doggy guests or active children, his cage will keep him out of the way and safe. Children should be firmly told not to put their fingers through the wire of the cage, nor should they tease or pester the dog.

Crating a dog can also help with house training – that is, teaching him to do his 'business' outdoors. Keeping him in a cage when you cannot watch him helps because he will be unwilling to dirty his bed, and keeping him confined keeps his insides calmer so that it becomes easier for him to 'hold on'.

SOCIALIZATION

As mentioned earlier, it is very important to socialize a puppy at an early age. He should be exposed to as many different situations, animals and people as possible. Once he has completed his inoculation period, he should be taken in the car as often as you can manage it. He should greet people and other dogs politely and without exuberance. While he is allowed to sniff dogs in what we call private places, he must learn that we humans do not find this acceptable at all. He must learn to have nothing to do with sheep, cattle, horses and poultry, and he should be gentle with cats and kittens. You may not like cats but other people do, and you can lose a lot of popularity if your dog chases or kills a friend's or host's cat or kitten.

People and Children

Try to arrange for your dog to meet children, but be sure that the children will comply with what you tell them. They should not run with, or from the dog, as this will end in tears because the puppy or dog is very likely to jump up at the child and nip it, damage its clothing or knock it over. Also I prefer that they do not play fetching games unless the child understands about the retrieve as it must eventually be performed. Mind you, it does not follow that how a dog behaves with a child is how he will behave with you, his pack leader.

Children must learn to keep their hands and voices down so as not to over-excite the dog, and they should not try to punish him until they understand when and how to do it. They should be encouraged to prepare the dog's food, and to give it to him, as this will help to give the dog a good impression of children. They should be shown how to stroke, pat and groom him. Once the dog has been trained to walk nicely on a slack lead, a child can be allowed to take him for a little walk, supervised.

Learning Not to Jump Up

It is very important that a puppy or a young dog learns at an early age not to jump up at people or children. Try gentle methods to begin with, such as stepping backwards as the puppy lifts his forefeet while saying 'Off!', and praising him when he puts his feet on the ground. With children or elderly people, you will need to intervene and be quite stern about it. A four-finger poke halfway down the side of the neck to push him off, accompanied with a sharp 'No!', should work. You may need to repeat this several times, but if you are consistent and firm he will understand, especially if you praise and stroke him once he is down, even if you need to hold him in a standing or sitting position. The main thing is to make him realize that 'Off' means 'Four feet on the ground', and that being on his hind legs is unacceptable and that you will make it unpleasant for him, whereas being on four feet is pleasant for him and therefore preferable.

In this day and age of political correctness we are not supposed to slap, but I have already said that this is not a book of political correctness. A slap does not have to be painful: it can give a dog a real surprise, which he will view as unpleasant and something to avoid in the future. You must never deliver a slap in temper. If you feel your temper rising, it is better to put the dog away in his quiet place until you have calmed down. You may worry that a slap will make a dog handshy, but a dog quickly realizes that your voice is a warning of what is to come, either nice or unpleasant.

With an older dog that has never learnt not to jump up, you may need to be quite tough. As he rises to put his feet on you, say 'No!' sharply, and push your palm firmly into the front of his muzzle. This should knock him off balance, but it is more a shock tactic than painful. Raising your knee to bump him in his chest as he comes up can be quite a shock to him, too. The idea is to give him an unpleasant bump, and not to hurt or harm him, so be very careful that your knee connects with his chest, and not below his ribcage. Do not be too fierce, and certainly do not knock the wind out of him. If you quickly follow up with 'Off!' in a kinder tone, and praise him when he has four feet on the ground, you may not need to repeat the treatment more than once or twice. However, although he may then be perfect with you, you may need to enlist the help of other people who are willing to correct the dog so that he understands that 'Off!' applies to everybody. Make sure that your assistants are no tougher than you are, but will take the matter seriously.

Now and then you find a dog that learns not to jump up at the front of people, but goes behind them and then jumps up. For this you need assistants who are willing and agile enough to spin round and show him he will be corrected whichever way he tries it.

Discouraging Inappropriate Sniffing
Inappropriate sniffing of people needs to be discouraged very firmly. It is socially acceptable amongst dogs for one to sniff the rear of another when meeting, but people do not appreciate it. Most of our training is going against a dog's instincts, so you are not being unkind in curbing this one. If your dog goes to push his nose between a person's legs, take him firmly by the scruff or collar and pull him firmly away, cover his muzzle with your hand, and rate him crossly while pushing him downwards. If this does not work, you will need to be harder on him. A quick cuff across the muzzle from you or the victim should

dissuade the dog. As in the case of jumping up, it is worthwhile enlisting the aid of other people to correct him so the dog realizes that he is not supposed to molest anyone.

Methods of Reprimand

A rolled-up newspaper, bound with sticking tape and kept to hand near the front door and other strategic places, is a useful tool. Just as you did with the muzzle-holding technique, it is worth teaching the dog about this tool in cold blood – that is, before he has done anything wrong. Take him by the collar and show him the rolled-up newspaper. Say 'No!' sharply but not loudly, and give him a tap or a smack – according to the toughness of the dog – with it, alongside the neck, or even, with the tough customer, alongside the muzzle. This will teach him that there is a physical accompaniment to 'No!', and in the future when he hears you say 'No!' and sees you reach for the rolled-up newspaper, he will show contrition and compliance. Make up with the dog after this lesson, then a few minutes later repeat it exactly as before. A human would find this confusing, but a dog will understand it clearly because he lives in the moment.

You could use the newspaper on the dog's flank or rump, but I think it is better that he sees where the punishment is coming from – that it is from you, his pack leader. If he does not see where it is coming from, he could associate the punishment with the thing he is looking at, which could be another person or dog, and it could make him afraid of, or aggressive, towards them.

Some people say that hitting is foreign to a dog, but this is not accurate. In life, for dogs as well as people, bad experiences do happen, and a dog may be knocked or hit inadvertently – for example a door may shut unexpectedly, a gate may swing to more quickly than expected, an item may roll off the table on to him, he may get under your feet so that you trip over him. When he is running with other dogs, one may change direction and run into him; when he is following another dog or human a branch may spring back in his face. The accidental hitting by inanimate or animate objects should make a dog more cautious as he goes about his business – the sting of the twigs teaches him to take more care when following. Being tripped over, bumped into or stepped on will make him more watchful about where he is in relation to people and other animals.

A human's instinct in attack or defence is to strike out; a dog's instinct in attack or defence is to bite. But just as a human can learn to modify his behaviour towards a dog in order to avoid being bitten, a dog can learn to modify his behaviour with regard to a human in order to avoid being hit. In my method of using the principle of 'either/or', he learns how to please us. He learns that actions bring consequences: in one instance, good consequences, in another, not so good. Of course, he has to learn what it is that pleases us and what displeases us, but it is up to us to get this across to him in ways that he can understand.

Those who think that we should not hit a dog say that hitting can lead to hand-shyness. In fact, just as we are intelligent enough to learn about the dog, he is intelligent enough to learn about us, at least in the context of his contact with us. Of course, we must still bear in mind that he lives in the moment. My opinion is that a dog knows the difference between your empty hand and your hand holding an object. He will learn that it is the object, in one case the rolled-up newspaper, which he must take notice of and respect. In other cases he will be delighted and excited by objects you have in your hand, such as his dinner, his grooming brush, or the lead which means that a walk is in the offing.

Play-biting can be a problem, especially when a puppy does it as their teeth are needle sharp! They do not mean any harm – they do it in play, just as they would with their siblings. When they bite their litter-mates it seldom hurts very much because, generally speaking, their skin is less sensitive than ours and they have a coat of fur. However, they do not realize that it hurts us quite a lot. I find that the best way of dealing with puppy-biting is to squeak in pain, which is probably what you would do anyway, and then pinch the puppy quite hard on the face or ear, again giving a sharp squeak. In this way he associates *your* squeak of pain with *his* pain. You may have to repeat this a few times, but he should catch on before long.

All dogs are different, and some are very soft and easily upset. You need to be careful with this sort – although interestingly, I find that the firmer I am with a dog, as long as I am fair, the more he appears to love me. In reality, this apparent adoration is just acceptance of authority. Our domestic dogs like to know who the pack leader is because it gives them a sense of security and confidence. Making a dog respect you, take a back seat to you – his pack leader – can overcome most of what we call training or behaviour problems.

Other Dogs

As mentioned above, sniffing personal places is normal amongst dogs: it is part of their greeting ritual. However, most of our 'training' involves curbing, channelling or redirecting certain of a dog's instincts; if you accept this, then you may agree that unwanted sniffing of other dogs is only acceptable in certain situations. There is a time and a place for everything.

When you and your dog are in the company of other dogs and their owners, such as at a shoot meet, the dogs will want to go through their sniffing ritual, and certain dogs, and bitches, may be over-enthusiastic about it and carry it a step further by, for example, mounting one another or showing aggression. This is not acceptable, and prevention is better than cure. Put your dog on a lead as you take him out of the car. As usual you should be vigilant, and as soon as you perceive him showing any interest in another dog, nip it in the bud with a stern word and a short, smart tug on the lead. Do not allow him to make the first pull, but check him before he makes a move, otherwise he may get into a situation where he is choking on the lead. He may well then associate the strangling feeling with the other dog, and this can lead to aggression.

Stock, Poultry and Cats

A gundog should be steady to all forms of temptation. This is achieved through training, and, as has already been said, training in so many instances is going

Linnet has had lessons to disabuse her of any interest in the hens. She is now focused on me.

against instinct. It is instinct that makes a dog want to chase prey and kill. With domestic animals and cats, this is not acceptable.

This subject is a matter of life and death for the dog as well as the victim. While a dog will seldom be put down for killing a cat, he will eventually be destroyed for chasing or killing cattle, sheep or poultry. Chasing doesn't always end directly in the death of the chased animal but it can, particularly in the case of sheep, lead to shock, abortion if in lamb, and, later, death.

With the puppy, the first time you see he is interested in looking at or watching stock, speak sternly to him and perhaps give him a slap on the muzzle. Then take him away and shut him up to 'think it over'. A cat will usually look after itself where a puppy is concerned, and give him a scratch or bite, which should be enough to alter his attitude. If the cat runs, however, you will need to treat the matter as unsteadiness, as with any other form of chasing: it is not allowed. I have always started to teach my puppies not to pay attention to stock from about three or four months. This has a useful side effect in that when they later see deer or rabbits running they know not to chase them – it's as if they think, 'Oh, that's just a fast sheep'. In fact the dog has learnt self discipline, which means that when he feels the urge to chase, he calms down and may even sit.

With a dog that has started to be dangerously interested in stock, you must act with absolute seriousness and without delay.

When you set out to disabuse a dog from an interest in stock or poultry, there are three rules you must keep. Let us assume that you start with a few chickens. The first rule is that you must keep an eye on the dog at all times. Once you have established where the chickens are, you can keep them in your peripheral vision without taking your eyes off the dog.

Second, you must never walk straight towards, or turn towards, the chickens. This would put you in hunting mode with the dog. Always walk at right angles or obliquely to the stock, and when you turn, turn away from the animals. To move straight towards them and then to punish him for showing interest will certainly confuse him. You want no confusion whatsoever.

Thirdly, when you see the smallest flicker of interest on the part of the dog, you must 'go for him' really furiously. You should have him on a check chain with a leather or soft fabric lead. When he cocks his ears or even looks toward the chickens, scold him fiercely and give him two or three rapid, severe jerks on the lead. He needs to feel that the situation is horrible – in fact so horrible that in the future, when he appreciates that he is in the presence of poultry, it is best for him to look at the clouds and say, 'Chickens? I can't see any chickens.'

Now, the next bit is very important indeed: you need to repeat the treatment at least three more times with different poultry, in different places – and the same goes for sheep, cows, horses, or any other stock in which the dog shows an unhealthy interest. He learns that the first hens are forbidden, but when he sees other hens in another location, he will think they are fair game. It goes under the rule that dogs learn in pictures, and what a dog sees is more important to him than what he hears. But when you have repeated the 'treatment' in three or four different locations, the penny should drop and the dog will realize that, 'Oh, it's not just the first chickens, or the second chickens – it's all chickens!'

As for cats, if the dog is not too aggressive and the cat will stay in the vicinity while the dog is loose, go up to the cat and stroke it and tell it how special it is. This is intended to raise the cat's status and show the dog that you hold the cat in high esteem, and that if you like and respect it, the dog should respect your opinion. Usually, if the cat is yours, each time you feed the cat, giving the dog a little food will make him begin to see the cat as a sort of ally.

The procedure is different if the dog is really out for blood. The cat will know it, so the training will probably have to take place indoors. Cats are inclined to scarper at the least sign of threat, and fences and walls are no hindrance to them. You will need to use a similar aversion method as for stock. Put the cat in a cage in a room to one side of and beyond the doorway. Bring the dog into the room on the check chain and leash, and walk past the cage. When you see the tiniest bit of interest, scold and jerk in a very serious way. Turn away from the cage and pass again, repeating the correction as necessary. Do this once more, then take the dog out of the room. The first session may not seem very satisfactory to you, as the dog may not capitulate to you, but if you then shut him away by himself for an hour, you should find him more co-operative on the next occasion.

Again, you will need to repeat the procedure in other places with the same cat and with other cats before you can feel confident that the dog will obey you.

Unfortunately, there are some dogs that have such a hatred of cats, they will never be absolutely steady to them and you will never be able to trust them. As a last resort, it could be that the electric collar would work, but most dogs learn that they only receive a shock when wearing the collar. Electric collars are an admission that proper, preventative training did not take place in the beginning. Prevention is always better than cure. Before resorting to this aid, be sure that the use of an electric collar is legal in your part of the world.

CAR TRAVELLING PROBLEMS

Car Sickness

It is pure misery for dog and owner alike when a dog doesn't travel well. Some just foam at the mouth and drool, and you cannot imagine how they can produce so much saliva. Some throw up as soon as the car starts to move, and some travel most of the way and then throw up just as you reach your destination.

Dogs are not sick in cars for the same reasons that we are. As soon as they gain a good association with being in the car and travelling, most cease to be sick or to drool almost spontaneously. Good associations can be built by various means. You could feed the dog his meals in the car. You could put him in the car and then give him a bone, leave him there to chew it for twenty minutes or so, then let him out but leave the bone in the car. After a few sessions like this you could start the engine, drive for ten yards then stop and leave him as before.

It seems to me, however, that as soon as a dog real-izes that it goes to nice places in the car, it stops being

a bad traveller almost straightaway. Very short journeys to meet a friend and go for a fun walk would be a very good way to build a nice association.

If your dog is used to being in a cage in the house, it will almost certainly help to have him in a cage in the car. This often solves the problem of car sickness because it restricts the dog moving about due to the motion of the car. It also restricts how much he sees of the passing landscape and other vehicles, and this may be beneficial. But the real reason I think it makes the dog travel better is that he is already used to being in a cage, and it is 'home' to him and makes him feel confident.

If it seems to be taking a long time for the dog to get over this problem, your veterinary surgeon should be able to help. A sedative which prevents the drooling and sickness can make the dog realize somehow that he does not have to be sick or upset.

Barking in the Car

This is a very annoying, distracting and sometimes alarming thing for a dog to do in the car. In fact it constitutes a dog being 'out of control' and is against the law, should you be driving at the time.

One day I stopped for petrol at a service station where it was not self-service. As the gentleman came to my window to ask what I required, the dog behind me lunged forwards to guard me and barked almost in my ear, making me jump nearly out of my skin. I rounded on the dog and gave him such a telling off, he never did it again – though he would sit in place and give a low growl. However, it is acceptable for a dog to guard you or the car, but there are various ways of doing everything.

Constant barking in a vehicle can be easily stopped with most dogs. Nipping it in the bud is best. Start with the dog outside the car. The dog does not have to be barking. Have a plastic cup of water or a water pistol, then say 'Be quiet' in a low but firm voice, and throw the water from the cup, or squirt the gun, at his face. Repeat this in two or three places, outside the car. An unpleasant but harmless association will be formed in connection with the phrase 'Be quiet'. Put the dog in the back of the car with the front windows open a few inches so he can hear you. When he begins to bark, say 'Be quiet' in the usual voice, and throw or squirt water straight at his face. Of course it will not splash him, it splashes the window between the two of you, but it will still have the desired effect. Then praise him for being quiet.

It is very important that you say the command in a low voice. If you raise your voice or shout, the dog could view this as you joining in and your job will be made harder.

If the dog barks while you are in the car, you should have an assistant with you in the early days of the cure. As soon as the barking begins, you say, 'Be quiet,' and your assistant turns around with the plastic cup or water pistol and shows it to the dog. If this is not enough, you may have to make a small sacrifice and allow a small amount of water to splash the interior of the car. It will be worth it. Later, it should be enough for you to raise the cup or pistol for the dog to see, while you continue driving safely, looking forwards.

This method can also be used to stop unnecessary barking in other situations, such as in the kennel or house.

Unfortunately there are some dogs that actually enjoy having water splashed in their face. With such a dog you can use the rolled-up newspaper, as in the teaching of household manners.

NERVOUSNESS

Nervousness is a fault of temperament which can be innate or learned. In either case, it can be an annoyance at best, and a danger to the dog or to people at worst. A nervous dog is difficult to train: he may run home when he receives the slightest hint of correction, he may run away at the sight of anything unusual, and may end up under the wheels of a car. He may even bite a person who extends a friendly hand.

A dog which is innately nervous can be a very difficult proposition, and in my experience, dogs are as likely as bitches to exhibit this fault. However, dog or bitch, if it is bred for work, you may find that when it is doing its job it blossoms.

Some dogs develop nervousness due to rough or unfair handling, but surprisingly commonly a dog can become exceedingly fearful through too much kind treatment. If a dog shows fear or anxiety at, say, a new situation, and the handler shows it a great deal of kindness, the dog is, in effect, being praised for showing nervousness. He is not being given confidence, nor any indication that he is in capable hands and that the handler is in charge and will protect him.

If a dog is praised for showing apprehension, he will learn that if he exhibits signs of fear, his handler will be nice to him. He can therefore 'train' his handler to be comforting and sweet to him, and may even be 'let off' the task in hand because the handler is afraid of scaring him – indeed he will soon become a consummate actor!

In this sort of situation, whether the nervousness is innate or learned, I am very firm with the dog. I have him on the lead and actually scold him for being afraid because he should consider that he is in my care and that I will look after him. I use the muzzle-holding technique together with cross words, and I let him know that I am affronted that he does not have faith in me. After an episode like this, I will shut him up just as I would after any training session to 'think things over' – that is, to let the physiology of learning work its way in his mind – and later in the day, or early next day, I will put the dog in the same or a similar situation again, treat him in the same way and shut him up afterwards.

When the dog begins to relax, you can actually feel the fear draining out of him. This is usually very soon, and I will offer him an edible reward. If he is still in a fearful state, he will not accept the treat. Eventually, if you continue to be stern with him, he will unwind enough to eat.

It is very important to treat this behaviour very firmly every time it occurs – and remain firm in your conviction: it will pay dividends.

AGGRESSION

I hold very strong views regarding aggression in dogs, especially that there is no place for an aggressive dog on any shooting day. It does not matter what the cause is: it is unacceptable for a dog to bite a human or another dog. A bite has to be in a dog to come out. Neutering may be the answer to the problem in some cases, but an aggressive Labrador should be discarded.

Some people will excuse a dog which is aggressive through nervousness, and I have discussed this above. If the methods described do not remove all traces of aggression, the dog should not be considered a suitable candidate for training as a gundog.

It is entirely unacceptable to breed from an aggressive Labrador.

There is one exception where you would excuse a dog for biting: occasionally, a dog bites because he is in extreme pain. One example might be when he becomes caught up in a wire fence. This commonly happens when he makes a mistake in jumping and puts one leg through the top strand on the start side of the fence and his body ends up on the other, so that all his weight hangs from the caught leg. This is very, very painful for him – he may yell and will struggle, and if you get near enough he will almost certainly bite you.

Act quickly: take your coat off and cover his head, then pitch his body back over the fence and this will usually free him. If the wire has become twisted around his leg, you will have to enlist help – one person to hold his weight up and the other to untangle him or to cut the wire if necessary. I carry a pair of wire cutters – part of my Leatherman tool – on my belt; I have only needed them a few times, but they have certainly repaid me for the bother of carrying them.

SEPARATION ANXIETY

'Separation anxiety' is a phrase sometimes used to account for the barking and destructiveness that occurs when a dog is left alone, though it can also occur when he has the company of other dogs. It usually happens when 'his' humans go and leave him. Some dogs can make a terrible fuss at being left by their owners because they consider themselves in charge of 'their' humans. When you go out, your dog may be very upset that he is unable to look after you. Part of the reason for this may be that the dog has not been made to realize his place in the pack – he has not been dominated in

a way he understands. He needs to be made to understand that you are in charge of him and of yourself (see Chapter 4, the section 'Dogs are Pack Animals').

Another reason for his being upset will be that he has not become gradually accustomed to your absence. All training should be done in small, easy-to-understand increments, and learning to be left alone is just another part of training.

When you first have your puppy or dog, make sure he is comfortable in your chosen place, give him a treat – and then leave him, shutting the door behind you, for two or three seconds. Go back and congratulate him, perhaps giving him another treat. If he is in a cage, let him out and make a fuss of him, then put him back. Leave him again for ten to twelve seconds and return as before, repeating the praise and letting him out. If, at any stage, when you close the door on him, he makes the smallest sound, go back, be very cross, and give him a small shake by the scruff, then leave him again for only a very short time so that you can get back to him before he starts to protest again.

Your aim is to be able to praise him for good behaviour, not to leave it so long that you have to scold him because he is noisy. Letting him out is a reward for quiet behaviour and shows him that it is not for ever, it is not prison, and you are the good guy who can open the door. I once had a dog called Bramley who would run into an open kennel unbidden just so I would ask him to come out again.

As with other matters of training, the dog will do what he finds preferable. Try to think of ways of making him realize that being quiet and calm when he is left alone will end well, will be preferable.

THE 'WRONG' DOG

If you do not seem to be making any progress with your dog, or he is exhibiting some fault which precludes him from making a good gundog, you must consider the options. Ask your instructor or someone whose opinion you value to give you an honest opinion of him.

All dogs are different. Some have the talent to make a good gundog; some do not. If your dog is persistently noisy, aggressive or intractable, you may have to accept that he is not the right material. Of course, you probably love him, 'warts and all', but see what your mentor thinks. Time is precious, and you should seriously consider replacing him with a more promising dog if that is what you are advised. Face up to the fact that it may be best either to re-home him or to consign him to being a pet.

Trying to train the 'wrong' dog will be exasperating: you will be irritated, frustrated and ashamed of your dog, and he will sense it and be unhappy. He will be happier with someone who does not expect so much from him. If he is aggressive, you must certainly consider whether it is right to pass him on, or whether it is best to have him put down. You certainly should not keep him, as he may attack your new dog or infect him with this undesirable trait.

If you do decide to have a new dog, take a lot of trouble to find the right one for you. It would be a huge knock to your confidence if you acquired another unlikely candidate. The right sort of dog will give you a lot of pleasure, and you will wonder why you persevered for so long with the wrong one. Re-homing the 'wrong' dog is not an admission of defeat: it is being realistic, and a dog which does not suit you may well be just the dog that someone else is seeking.

CHAPTER 6

PREPARING FOR TRAINING

WHEN TO START

A young Labrador can learn a surprising number of words, but until he is physically mature he should not be expected to jump fences or do long retrieves. Any prolonged or repeated stress on the joints may lead to dysplasia and thus to irreversible damage, lameness and arthritis. A puppy will usually attain his full height at around ten months of age, although a male may grow on for a few weeks longer. After this, dogs fill out and become more mature in appearance. They can concentrate for longer periods of time and can perform more strenuous activities.

I have often noticed that a Labrador puppy of the right breeding will suddenly start to pay more attention to me, even when I am not trying to do something with him. It is almost as if he is asking, 'Can we do something today? I want to start something new.' I look upon this as a pivotal moment. It can come at around five months or later, but not usually before that. It may not come at a convenient time, but it should not be ignored. Even if you only have time to give him a few minutes of attention – an arm round his shoulder and a few kind words – this will greatly benefit your relationship.

Part of your decision about when to start should be based on how much time you have to devote to the dog's training. I find that in the shooting season I have very few daylight hours to spare, so I tend not to commence a young dog's training programme then. Better to leave it until the season is over and there is more time available to work out a proper timetable of regular sessions. The days will be lengthening and the weather improving.

This is not to say I do nothing with my youngster during the shooting season. Whenever I have the chance, I spend time 'bonding' with him and getting him to focus on me by doing very short training sessions, often indoors.

KEEP A DIARY

If you keep a diary of brief but legible and clear comments of your training sessions, I think you will be surprised and pleased, over time, with your dog's progress. Every trainer will reach a point, probably with every dog, when he despairs that he has made a mistake or that progress is nil. If you have kept a diary, check back and you will usually find it will give you fresh heart.

YOUR ATTITUDE

Your attitude is of primary importance. You should be positive when dealing with your dog without being rough or bullying. He must feel that you are someone he should and can look up to, in more ways than one. To train effectively, you have to take the place of his 'pack leader'. This means that you must seldom be wrong, and therefore must always be thinking ahead, planning and being alert to possible pitfalls. Timing is crucial and requires a high degree of concentration, so if you are 'out of sorts', tired, hungry, thirsty or uncomfortable, leave the training until you are feeling better and can give of your best.

Although a dog can learn a great deal through his senses – that is, by association – he cannot learn as we can by reading, nor can he derive any benefit from lectures or advice. His learning of the meaning of words is therefore entirely up to his trainer. You, the trainer, have to get your meaning across to the dog, and direct

the course and progress of the training. To do this you must go to his level, by which I mean that you must always try to see things the way your dog sees them – he hasn't the intellect to guess how your mind works. His learning is limited to connecting cause and effect, and to realizing that pleasing you has 'survival value' and will bring him pleasure. So, as has been said before, it is your job to get on to his 'wavelength' so that he in turn can understand you.

Do not be tempted to skip any step, but always be thorough. It is rather like building a house of cards: if you follow each step carefully, you will succeed, but if you leave out parts of the process, it will all be weakened. You can build on success, but you cannot build on failure, so you should expect the best and try to achieve it. This means that your attitude should be positive, looking for the good, and not tolerating behaviour you find unacceptable.

Dogs are very quick in acting and reacting, and if we are to impress them, we must also be quick. We need to be quick with praise and quick with correction. You must never hesitate to correct in the hope that the dog will come right. Imagine that you are driving your car along a narrow lane and you come round a bend to find a lorry parked across the road. Do you do nothing in the hope that the lorry will just disappear? Certainly not. You do something. You act! Immediately! Ignoring your non-responding dog does not have the dire consequences that ignoring the obstructing lorry might have, but if you act positively and promptly when he does not obey you, you will make good progress with his training.

Equally, if you praise him the instant you see a good response, progress will be accelerated. It's a balancing act. Training should be all about either/or for your dog: either he is doing what you require and is praised, or he is disobeying you and therefore will be admonished and corrected.

There will be times when you find that you are not getting through to your dog. He may be distracted by something – there are many smells he can perceive, such as a bitch in season, of which we have no idea at all. He may be brewing up for an illness. He may be hot, or hungry or thirsty, or you may have fed him too recently. He may just be having an off day. When this happens you may think he is being dim or stubborn, but do not, on any account, become angry. Anger may lead to harshness, and this will cause fear, and a dog cannot learn when he is in a fearful state. Anger gives you a knot in the stomach, and when you have that, even if the dog eventually performs the exercise, you will not be able to bring yourself to praise him sincerely and immediately as you should.

If you feel that you are becoming frustrated, have the willpower to change your plan. Stop trying to teach the exercise that is causing the problem, and choose something simple that you know the dog can do well. Ask him to do that, praise him, and put him away in his quiet place. You must always end on a good note so that the dog is left with a good impression of you and will be happy to come out with you the next time.

Ultimately you are seeking a team-mate, so even while maintaining your 'top dog' status, your outlook can still be friendly, even at times conspiratorial. Working a gundog is a sport in its own right, and a sport should be fun. You are aiming for a high standard, but both of you can, and should, enjoy it.

CRIME AND PUNISHMENT

In preparation for training a dog it is important to have decided upon your attitude regarding correction and punishment. In a perfect world you would be so careful and forward-thinking that most of the time you would only need to praise, and your dog would be so soft and compliant that any punishments could be of the mildest kind. However, life is not like that: we are fallible, and most dogs are forever looking for ways to receive more attention from us. I think that sometimes they will do an exercise badly so that we will correct them and go over it again, thereby giving them more attention.

In these days of political correctness, even the word 'punishment' is frowned upon. But let's look at the facts. A dog is a dog, not a human. We cannot change his instincts or his way of learning in the way that we humans have changed, and are still changing and controlling our attitudes. Political correctness is a concept for humans, and it cannot work with dogs. If we are to get our ideas and wishes across to a dog, we must be practical, and must approach the subject from his way of understanding. If this book is to do anything, I hope and intend that it will cause trainers and handlers to be more observant, more consistent, fairer and more humane. I hope it will help handlers to understand their dog.

What should be considered a crime? In an untrained or a trained dog, such things as jumping up on us, getting on the furniture, stealing our food, chewing our belongings, digging up the garden, taking washing off the line and, play-biting just come naturally to him, but these behaviours are unacceptable to us. Nevertheless the dog does not know he is 'wrong' – he is just following his feelings. We have to teach him what is, and what is not, acceptable to us.

In a trained dog we might consider it a crime when the dog goes against training and against what he has been taught. He may know perfectly well that he should not jump up on people, pull on the lead, run-in or chase, but now and then he does it just the same. He does it because his instinct or desire is stronger than his training, so the misdemeanour is the preferable thing to him. He has, at some time, found his handler to be imprecise or inconsistent, and inconsistent correction leads to inconsistent obedience. He doesn't think of the consequences because he lives in the present. He doesn't think, 'Oh, it's worth it,' because he does not think of the future. After the event he does not think of the past, however recent: he lives in the present. However, he has memory. He will see your cross expression, your body language, and hear your angry voice. He remembers what they mean and he will appear to be contrite. You will think that he knows he was wrong.

So often have I heard 'He knew he had done wrong' – but I would contend that no, he didn't. He knew from your body language that you were cross, but he did not, I assure you, know why. In other words, he recognizes that you are angry, and he knows what that means you might do to him, physically, but he does not have the intellect to put it together in his mind with the misdemeanour he recently committed.

Dogs live in the moment, and have little concept of the past or future, so it is useless to praise or punish before or after an event. Praise and correction must take place at the moment the dog is pleasing or displeasing you. Then he will connect his action – or non-action – with the consequences.

I know I am repeating myself, but I think this bears repeating. In the wild pack, if a dog does wrong, the pack leader or his mother will let him know in no uncertain terms and immediately that his behaviour is unacceptable. Everything is black or white; there are few grey areas, if any. It is an either/or world.

If a dog does something you don't like, you must act immediately to make him know that what he has done will not be tolerated. For example, if he jumps up at you, raise your knee to bump him in the chest and say 'No!' sharply as you connect with him. Then say 'Off' in a kinder tone, meaning 'Feet on the ground'. You must be careful not to wind the dog or injure him – it is just to make it very unpleasant so that he never wants to jump up at you again. However, this doesn't mean he won't do it to other people, so you must enlist help from other strong-minded friends who will give him the same treatment and who also know that they must not harm

the dog. They must just make jumping up unpleasant. To be fair, you or the other person should say 'Off' to warn the dog before he goes to jump up. This gives him a choice – either/or.

If, however, the dog commits a misdemeanour when you are not present, such as spending a penny on the carpet, you must consider it your fault in not giving him the chance to do his business when he needed to, and you certainly cannot punish him, because time has elapsed since the act occurred. Only if you catch the dog in the act can you punish and correct.

And what should you do when a trained dog has done something wrong? First you should ask yourself if the disobedience was deliberate, or did you make a sound or a movement that he took to mean that he should act? Running-in is frequently the result of a word or an action which the dog mistook for the licence to go. Or was it a case where the dog did not fully understand the command? All too often a dog disobeys because he hasn't been properly taught the command. Ask yourself, 'Have I been inconsistent?' Be honest with yourself, and if you believe that any of this is true, go back over the teaching of the exercise right from the very beginning. In this way you can be sure that if the dog goes wrong again, he is not co-operating with you. If this is the case, you must show him that you mean what you say and that you will follow through.

Do not be harsh. Harsh training may give you obedience when the dog is within reach, but that does not mean he will work well when out of sight. Harshness can also make a dog fearful and therefore tense, and a tense dog will take longer to learn something than a relaxed, trusting one.

Some trainers and books will tell you that the way to punish a dog is to grip him by the loose skin on either side of his neck and lift him off the ground, scolding severely. In my opinion this is entirely wrong. 'Up', in anybody's language, is where we all want to be, dogs included. We humans want to rise in the social scale, to go 'up the ladder': in school we wanted to be top, and in our job we want to improve, to go up through the ranks, gain a higher salary. Similarly a dog, even if he is pack member material, will still want to be top dog. Lifting a dog up, even though you may be rating him fiercely at the time, is confusing. It is also bad for your back!

If a dog were to step out of line in the pack situation, the leader would never, ever lift him up: he would attack him from above and get him down on the ground. Then, according to the seriousness of the misdemeanour, he might just growl and hold him down for several seconds, or he might give him a good shaking. The human leader must do much the same in order to show the dog that he will not tolerate disobedience. What I find most effective is to push the dog down with one hand gripping his scruff or collar and the other hand performing the muzzle-holding technique.

All dogs are different, and to impress a soft dog may only require that you rest your hand across his muzzle for a few seconds, speaking firmly to him. It is so important to assess your dog's character accurately. If you are too forceful with a gentle-natured dog you could make him very fearful of you, and as has been said before, a dog cannot learn in a fearful state.

A strong-minded dog may need to be pushed right down to the ground by the collar, and your other hand must hold his muzzle for the whole time. How long you keep him there is determined by the seriousness of the crime and how well he accepts your dominance. When you let him up, you must do so slowly. If he doesn't seem to be taking you seriously, let him think you are going to let him up, then change your mind a time or two and push him down again, scolding him sincerely but not loudly.

I frequently have pupils who are reluctant to use physical punishment on their dog in the belief that it will damage their relationship with him. If this is what you think, I believe it will help you if you remember, as I have said earlier, that you are very unlikely ever to hurt a dog more than he will be hurt in play with another dog. Our Labradors give of their best and are actually happiest when their handler adopts the pack leader role. To gain and maintain this position, you have to be tough now and then.

Do not shout at any time. You should not have a sore throat after any training session. A cross voice does not have to be loud – it is remarkable how acute a dog's hearing is. It is not the decibels that matter to a dog – it is how you make him feel. If you have embarrassed him or caused him some discomfort, in tandem with your cross voice, he will try to avoid making you cross.

Your voice, body language and general demeanour must change according to the dog's behaviour. You must be like Jekyll and Hyde: one second you are pleasant, fondling and gentle; the next stern, firm and correctional. I have been at the point of saying crossly 'Naughty dog!', with my tongue already on the 'N', but have had to change my tone and words to a genuine 'Nice dog, very good!'.

A repeated warning here: you may often see what looks like an expression of defiance on a dog's face, but it is not defiance – it is lack of understanding. So do be careful, and be sure what your dog's expression means. If you act in haste, you may damage your relationship with him, and this damage will take much time to undo. When you see this expression, it means you need to go back to the 'drawing board' and start again: begin at the beginning, and don't leave the exercise until you are sure that the dog understands. Do not become exasperated because you think he should understand and respond: it may take several sessions before you see that he has grasped what you mean, but you will reap the benefit because he will have an accurate and lasting understanding of what you want.

Occasionally you might ask a dog to do something that you know full well he does understand – for example, to go into his kennel – and he looks dim and goes the other way. This can be seen by you to be blatant disobedience, but you should ask yourself, 'Have I done something recently to make him not want to go in?' It may be that last time you returned from an outing, you invited him into the house with you for a while. He enjoyed that, and now he is saying that he would like that as an alternative to going into the kennel. Especially in the case of a puppy, I would commend his intelligence – but all the same, you should insist that he goes into the kennel. Go in with him, and give him a treat to make it all worthwhile. With repetition, he will accept the fact that you make the choices, but that it is not so bad when you choose the less attractive option.

On the other hand, he may be refusing to go in because of something unpleasant that happened to him when he went into the kennel previously. Try to find out what it might have been: perhaps another dog bullied or bit him, perhaps he hurt himself somehow – you may never know. Do what you can to eliminate any possible problems, and then, if you are firm but kind and give him an edible reward, you will get him over it.

However, as has been said earlier, do not be slow, do not hesitate in hope, do not coax or cajole with words – put a lead on him and physically make him do what you want. In this case, it would be to go into the kennel. Make him go in, then reward him. You should not be rough, just firm, and after you have once had to physically make him do something, put a flat, non-tightening collar on him so it is easy to take hold of him if you need a repeat performance. If he avoids you and will not be caught, a piece of baler twine about half a metre long attached to the collar should make it possible for you to arrest him without frightening him.

This is how I would deal with many examples of perceived disobedience. Give the dog the benefit of the doubt, but be assertive. Your aim is to make what you want preferable to anything else.

EQUIPMENT

In the beginning you will not need much, but it is advisable to have what I consider the basic necessities.

Collar and Lead

It is strange, if you think about it, that we lead a dog by the neck, but most of us take it for granted that this is what to do. We humans would not like it one bit – it makes us think of slaves at best and the hangman at worst. In fact for dogs it is not so strange. Because the pack leader dog uses the neck area to administer punishment, pack member dogs are accustomed to pressures, even bites, on the neck. Furthermore, the neck area is used by dogs to rag and drag each other in their rough games. Over thousands of years, the dog's neck area has become gradually less and less sensitive. This is why we can grip and hold a dog by the scruff without it seeming to hurt him. And how convenient for us that a collar fits on his neck almost as if it were made for our use.

You will need both a collar and a lead. Many people use a rope slip-lead, but I do not think this is suitable for training. For a dog's initial training, I prefer to use a check chain and a leather or soft nylon lead with a trigger clip. When your dog is word perfect at heel you can use a rope slip-lead, but make sure it is soft and pliable and fits easily into a pocket.

There are several reasons I prefer to use the check chain. One is that the chain makes a noise when it is tightening and warns the dog, so that after a few corrections he will hear the first few links run through and correct himself. Another reason is that you can detach the lead from the chain during the transition from working on the lead to off lead, and the dog still feels under a degree of control. The clip of the lead should be big enough and easy enough for you to operate with one hand. Keep the metal clip in your hand when the lead is off the dog so that it cannot accidentally hit him.

The collar should never be called a choke chain, nor should it ever be used to choke a dog: its correct use is merely to check the dog and cause momentary discomfort, and most of the time it should be completely loose and comfortable on his neck. The two round rings of the collar should lie together; it should have medium-sized links but no swivel. Swivels interfere with the free-running of the chain through the ring. The collar should fit comfortably around your dog's neck just above the point of the shoulder. The length of check chains is measured by the imperial system from the outside of the round rings at either end. A 22 or 24in (56 or 61cm) chain will fit most Labradors, although a very big dog will, of course, need a longer one.

There is a right way and a wrong way to put on the collar. Holding one of the round rings in one hand, let the chain hang down. Take the lower ring in your other hand and allow the chain to run through it to form the slip loop. If, for instance, you are going to have your dog at heel on your left, you will need the ring that runs on the chain to come from the underside of his neck. The lead is attached to the other ring, and you should endeavour to keep the clip and the rings resting together at the base of the right side of the dog's neck. When tension is put into the lead and then released, gravity will loosen the chain. However, if the collar is put on with the running ring coming over the dog's neck, when the lead is tightened and then released, it will not be able to loosen.

As a point of technique, when you take the chain off the dog, clip the lead on to both rings of the collar so

LEFT: The correct way for the check chain to be put on if the dog is walked to heel on your left. After being tightened, gravity will loosen the chain when the lead is loosened.

ABOVE: Assembling a check chain. Holding one ring in your hand, drop the links of the chain through it and attach the clip of the lead to the free ring.

LEFT: The wrong way. If the ring that runs on the chain comes over the dog's neck, it will not loosen when tension is removed from the lead.

When you remove the chain from the dog's neck, clip the lead on to both rings to keep the collar intact, ready for the next time you wish to use it.

that the chain is ready for its next use. This saves so much fiddling about when you take the lead and chain out of your pocket to put it on the dog again.

Your lead is an 'off switch'. Once you have finished an exercise satisfactorily, put the lead on. It prevents the dog from doing anything which might make him forget the lesson, and it helps him relax because he is under your physical control and therefore does not have to make decisions. A relaxed dog will take in his lessons well.

When you put your lead away, always put it in the same place. I put it in my left jacket pocket. Please do not put it around your neck! Do not drop it on the ground, either – you may need to go out to your dog and put the lead on to correct him. If you use a check chain, remember to clip the lead on to both rings when you take it off the dog so as to keep the loop intact. When you place it over the dog's head, just move the clip to the ring which allows the chain to slip. If you use a rope slip-lead, make sure the loop is kept open and big enough to go over the dog's head before you put it in your pocket. See how it looks, and you will soon become adept at putting it on the dog quickly.

Whistles

You will need a whistle. A whistle disturbs game less than the human voice, it carries further, and it can be more consistent – though naturally it can vary in intensity and length of toot or blast according to the mood of the person blowing! Care should be exercised in this department! The black plastic sort shaped a bit like a torpedo is easy to use and can be readily replaced. These come in several different pitches, denoted by a number on the back of the whistle, and some have a pea inside them. I prefer the $211\frac{1}{2}$ as it does not have a pea – they sometimes get stuck – and the pitch is low enough for me to hear, therefore I can be sure that the dog is hearing it too.

The metal 'silent' whistle is not a good idea in my opinion. If the pitch is set so high that you cannot hear it, you cannot be sure that when the dog disobeys you it has actually heard the whistle. You can set the whistle so that you can hear it, but in cold weather you stand the risk of having the metal sticking to your lips!

The length of the lanyard of your whistle is important. The whistle should hang mid-chest so that it does

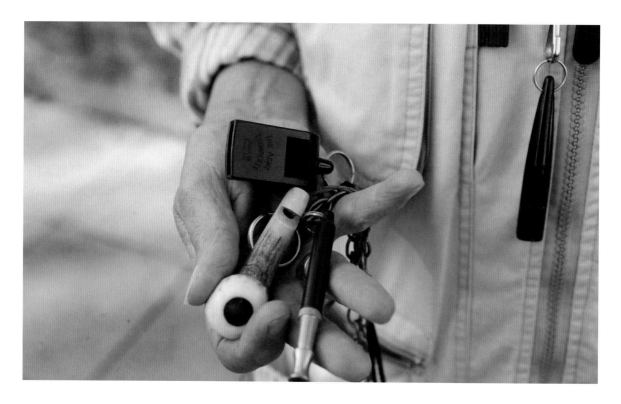

A collection of whistles. The one on the far right (hanging from my neck) is my preferred type.

not dangle in your dog's face when you bend over to take a retrieve. This may also possibly save you from ingesting germs or worm eggs, because the whistle does not come into contact with the dog so readily.

As soon as you acquire your whistle, put it on a lanyard and decide where it should be kept. I recommend that you have a couple of spares, and that one hangs on a certain hook in the house, and another perhaps on the gearstick of your car, or in the pocket of your game bag. I lay the lanyard of the third one across my hairbrush so that when I do my hair in the morning I see it and put it on.

Retrieve Articles

You will need a selection of dummies and other articles for your dog to retrieve. You will need at least four articles so that you keep your dog's interest. If you keep throwing the same dummy over and over, even the keenest dog will eventually get fed up and either start to play with it or refuse to retrieve. It appears to him that you do not value the dummy because you throw it away every time he brings it, so why should he value or respect it? On the other hand, a few dogs which are only ever given one dummy to retrieve, over and over, think that that is the only one they should retrieve, and will refuse to pick anything else.

I find tennis balls very useful, so have four of them as well. Make sure everything is marked with your name, and that similar dummies are numbered so that you can tell them apart. In the olden days we used to make our own dummies out of socks and anorak sleeves stuffed with a variety of fillings, but now dummies of all materials and shapes can be bought relatively cheaply. There are many gundog training equipment websites, and you will find that they stock many weird

A collection of retrieve articles. The black ball (far right) is painted with a white mark which looks very much like a rabbit's scut when the ball is rolled on the ground, and is very enticing to a dog.

and wonderful kinds of dummy. You will have to decide which you think will be practical, and which are just plain silly.

Pistols and Launchers

Many people find a starting pistol useful to accustom a dog to the sudden loud noises he will encounter on a shoot day. However, many dogs are upset by the sharp crack of a pistol, even dogs that are happy with the report of a 12-bore shotgun, so to begin with the pistol should be fired at a good distance away from the dog. Dogs quickly learn the connection between a bang and a retrieve, and this usually helps them overcome any anxiety. You will need an assistant to fire the pistol so that you can be with the dog and see his reactions. As long as the dog shows acceptance, the pistol can gradually be brought closer. (*See* Chapter 10, the section halfway through the chapter 'Introduction to Gunfire'.)

A dummy launcher is part of my training equipment, but I feel it has limited use, partly because in 'real life' the bird does not come from the gun. Launchers use a .22 blank cartridge to propel a canvas-covered or plastic dummy from thirty to a hundred yards, according to the load of the blank. Most dogs find the launcher very exciting, so it can be an aid in teaching steadiness. Like the pistol, it also makes a sharp crack, and many dogs are not happy about it although most learn to tolerate it because the reward for enduring the sound is a retrieve.

The person firing the device should wear ear defenders unless a very light load of blank is used. There is a type of launcher which allows one or more tennis balls to be fired; this simulates the event of more than one bird being shot at the same time, and helps teach the dog to mark more than one fall.

The Americans have invented a remote-controlled dummy launcher which can fire a number of dummies. These are expensive, but their usefulness is undoubted, as instructors can remain with their pupils and fire the apparatus at impressive distances, all without having to tolerate the noise at close quarters.

A game bag with the dummies arranged upright so that a different one can be extracted for each retrieve.

Game Bag

You will need a game bag at some point, and better sooner than later. Do not buy a huge one or one day you will find that everyone else is letting you carry their equipment! Mine measures 11in high by 15in wide by 5½in deep. It has two pockets and a net across the front, a divider in the middle, and a zipped pocket across the back. Many people favour the 'training vest' which has back and front pockets and distributes the weight equally across your shoulders.

Clothing and Footwear

It is important to be comfortable: you must be able to concentrate, so you must not be distracted by any sort of discomfort. Wear comfortable clothing: it must be warm enough or cool enough. It must not be too tight, and it must be tidy and fastened so as not to flap in the dog's face. If you need to wear a scarf, in the same way make sure the ends are not dangling in the dog's face or obscuring your own: it is vital that you can see your

A training vest. An advantage of the vest is that it distributes the weight of the dummies and other equipment evenly.

dog and that he can see you. Your footwear must be comfortable and appropriate to the weather and terrain. If you need to wear gloves, make sure they are the sort that you can work in. They should be a pale colour so that your hands appear much as they would unclad.

Whatever you wear, have pockets that you can put a lead into or take a biscuit out of easily. Pockets are indispensable. You must be able to free your hands when you are training or working a dog. I absolutely hate to see people put leads around their own neck; it reminds me of the hangman. It is convenient and quick to put a lead into use if all you need do is fish it out of your pocket.

The Quiet Place

An essential aspect of preparation is to have the proper sort of quiet place to put your dog when you have finished each training session. The dog should have the minimum of items to interest or distract him – no toys, food or bones, and little or nothing to see or hear. A cage in your car or utility room is good. The car cage, usually called a transit box, should have opaque sides and back walls; it should be well ventilated, but not made entirely of wire – in other words, the dog should have minimum viewing facility. A kennel away from other animals without a view is also good. He should have been accustomed to the quiet place from an early age, and should view it as a pleasant place to be (see Chapter 2).

PLAN YOUR TRAINING SESSIONS

Before you even pick up your equipment, be sure to give some thought to what you hope to achieve in the training session. Have a plan, remembering that the optimum period of time for a lesson is six minutes.

Do not feed your dog before a training session: he will be sharper and keener if he is a little bit hungry. If he has just been fed it is best to let him stay quietly digesting his food.

Start every training session with the dog on the lead. Do some heelwork, first on the lead, then off. If he is not going well, return him to the lead. If you do this, you are physically in control and will be able to make him

do it right and therefore be able to praise him. Being able to praise accelerates progress.

Timing is crucial: your correction must be given immediately something starts to go wrong, and equally, your praise must be given immediately you see the response you want.

Always end a session on a good note. If things have not gone according to plan or not well at all, nevertheless always finish by asking the dog to do something he can do well, even something as simple as the 'sit'; then praise him and put him away. If you do this, the dog's last impression of the training session is a good one, and he will be happy when he goes out for the next one. If you leave him with a bad impression, he will not look forward to the next time.

POINTS OF TECHNIQUE

I wish I had a pound for every time I have said each of the following: 'Put your lead away', 'Free your hands', 'Watch your dog' and 'Have your whistle ready'.

When you take the lead off, always put it in the same pocket so that you can take it out quickly when you need it. You must have the lead readily to hand: if your dog goes wrong, you should be able to take the lead out in a flash to put it on him. And if you are using a check chain, remember to put the leash clip on both rings when you take it off the dog so that the loop is intact and ready to go over his head when needed.

You must have your hands free when you are working a dog because you will need to give hand signals. You will also need to be able to take delivery of the retrieve unencumbered by anything in your hands: therefore free your hands.

Another point I frequently find myself making is, 'Watch your dog; the dog will watch the dummy.' If you are concentrating on your dog you can detect the smallest sign that he is going to do the wrong thing and correct him. Consistent correction leads to consistent obedience. Whether you are throwing the dummy yourself or someone else is throwing for you, watch your dog. The fact that you are not able to mark the dummy because you are watching the dog is not as important as keeping the dog steady. In fact, you should be able

Sending for a retrieve: this is the correct way, side view, to prepare to cast your dog out for a retrieve. You have put your lead away so your hands are free. You have established the direction in which you wish the dog to go, so now fix your eyes on the dog's head to ensure that he is looking that way. Have your whistle ready in your mouth or, if you prefer, in your left hand. Place your sending hand alongside and close to the dog's muzzle, pointing in the direction you want him to go.

Sending for a retrieve: correct, front view. You are ready to cast your dog. Make sure that he is focused on the line you wish him to take.

Sending for a retrieve: incorrect, side view. The handler is not looking at the dog, the whistle is not ready and the dog is not looking in the right direction. If the dog is cast now, the handler will almost certainly have to correct or restart him.

Sending for a retrieve: incorrect, front view. The dog and handler are not connected, let alone focused on each other. If the dog is given the retrieve command he will almost certainly go wrong.

to hear roughly where the dummy lands, and of course your dog is looking there even if you aren't.

When casting your dog out, make sure you look at him, then you can see that he is looking where he is supposed to be going. Before you cast him, look where the retrieve is, establish in your mind where you are going to send him, then keep your eyes on his head and your casting hand to see that they correspond.

If you have your eye on your dog as much of the time as possible, you will see those tiny indications which tell you what he is thinking of doing before he does it. It may be the flick of an ear, a change in his eye, a turn of his head, the raising or dropping of his tail, a tension in his body. Watching him when he is working will tell you if he has found scent or is about to get into difficulty. You will see the right moment to blow the stop or recall whistle and when to give the 'Hunt' command.

Before you even think of sending your dog out on a retrieve, put your whistle in your mouth. If your casting command begins with 'B', 'P', 'F', or any sound that will make you blow your whistle, you will probably have to hold it in the hand that you do not use to cast the dog. Even words such as 'Ripple', 'Dapple', 'Away', 'Out' can make you blow your whistle inadvertently. Practise saying the words you intend to use as names and commands with the whistle in your mouth and see what happens. If you blow your whistle by mistake in this way, you are, in effect, saying 'Stop' when you may well mean 'Go'.

Regarding the use of the whistle: make sure that you keep to the signal you have chosen, and do not alter the length or intensity of the toot because you think it will have more effect. Do not be like some Americans who believe that more is better, and that too much is not enough – with dogs, more is just different and therefore not recognizable.

CHAPTER 7

ABOUT COMMANDS

What do we mean when we talk about training a dog? I suppose that basically it is teaching the dog the meaning of the sounds we use in making our language, in this case English. It means conveying what we want the dog to do for us in response to words, signals and whistle sounds. The trained dog has been taught to act or position himself in response to a hand or whistle signal or verbal command from his handler.

Dogs can become very clever at picking out sounds they know – many dogs can pick out a single word in the middle of a sentence. I taught my first Labrador, Christy, to push a door shut on the command 'Shut'. Very soon I could say to her, 'Oh, Christy, you've left the door open; would you please shut it,' and she would go to the door and close it with her paw.

Christy – my first Labrador – at four years.

THE FOUR KEY COMMANDS

Whether you are training a gundog, guide dog or guard dog, I believe there are four basic commands and all the rest hang on these. They are 'Sit', 'Come', 'Heel' and 'Run on'.

'Run on' is my release command and it means 'Suit yourself, within reason'. It does not mean 'Leave the county': it means that the dog may break the last command given, or not. For example, if you have told him to sit, he should sit indefinitely. However, if you give your release command, he may stand up if he wants to, or indeed he may choose to remain in the sit position – he may sit if he likes, stand up if he likes or run about if he likes. Having said that, if he is on the lead, he must not pull on it; the collar and lead are your property and he should not pull on them. Other words and phrases you could use include 'Off you go', 'Away', and 'Free'. 'Okay' and 'All right' are not good as we say these words so freely and often and without even thinking. The release command needs to be special, a word or phrase that we use consciously.

'Sit' is the keystone to all training. If your dog will sit instantly and steadily whenever and wherever he is told, he is under control. For a gundog, however, 'Sit' means much more than just that he should assume a physical position. It comes to mean, 'Stop and pay attention to me, I am going to show you something interesting.' So early on, you must make it more than just a pure discipline: you should give him lots of praise for sitting to command, and quite soon you should start showing him things that are interesting to him as soon as he sits. Later, when he learns the 'Sit' whistle – or 'stop' whistle as it is often called – he must quickly learn that it will lead to you helping him to find the retrieve.

Possibly equal in importance to the 'Sit' is the command 'Come'. If your dog will turn on his heel the moment he hears this command, he will be an asset, not a liability. There are many occasions when a dog must come to you, even if he has found something more interesting, and early on you must be thinking of ways to make coming to you preferable to anything else.

If your dog will remain reliably at 'Heel' in spite of all distractions, without you having to check on him, you can be relaxed with him and justifiably proud of him.

HOW DOGS UNDERSTAND WORDS

To a dog, human words, even his name, are just sounds which at first have no meaning for him. Through giving him a physical association, we teach the dog the meaning of words. However, initially that meaning is only associated by the dog with the pronunciation, the tone, the level of decibels, and the voice of the speaker; another person saying the same word or words, even the name of the dog, will not at first be understood. Over time and with frequent contact with his trainer and other people who need to manage the dog, he will learn that words, even though they sound different, mean the same thing. What clever creatures they are! They can learn a foreign language! They can learn accents and intonations, whispering and shouting.

Obviously it will make learning easier for the dog if you can always say your commands in the same way in the early stages of training – in other words, be consistent. It is not always easy to do this, however; for example, your dog may be slow to understand a certain facet of training, you may become irritated and your voice will change. However, if you are aware of this and are willing to try another way, you will be able to control your voice; you can train yourself to do it right.

You only need one command for one thing, but that command can cover a meaning which would take a human several words to explain to another human. For example, the word 'Sit' means just that, but to a dog it should also mean, 'Assume the sit position and remain in it until released or directed to do something

else.' There is no question about the meaning. No other word should be used, nor is any other word necessary. We humans use many words when speaking to each other, often whole sentences meaning just one thing. We call it reinforcement. For example, we might say to a person, 'Sit down there, don't move, wait until I tell you what to do next.' A human will understand all that. But with a dog, if you use more than one word for one thing, believe me, the dog will think you are offering him a choice. So, for instance, you should not say, 'Sit, stay' because it is confusing: you might as well say a whole sentence, and if you did, you would have to teach the dog that all the words mean just the one thing: 'Sit'.

Of course, a dog can learn that two or more words mean the same thing but it will take correspondingly longer to teach the extra commands than it does to teach one.

Things do become slightly contradictory as time goes on because you will need to teach the dog that some of the voice commands have a corresponding hand and whistle signal. Having a hand signal to accompany a voice command is very helpful because of the fact that what a dog sees is so much more important to him than what he hears. As I have said earlier, dogs are very short-sighted. They have difficulty distinguishing stationary shapes – that is why if you put on a coat he has not seen before and a funny hat, he may bark suspiciously at you. His appreciation of movement, however, is extremely acute – he can spot a running rabbit's scut bobbing along at 150 yards! So your signals must have, at best, a slight but distinct movement in them.

As I have said earlier, we use the whistle because it carries further than the human voice, and I believe it disturbs game less. We can also be more consistent with whistle signals than perhaps we might be with the voice.

In order to learn to respond to a command, the dog needs to be physically positioned in the first few instances. For example, in the case of 'Sit', we use our hands and the lead to position him whilst giving the command and when the dog is in the sitting position, we repeat the word, praise and pat him, perhaps give him an edible reward. With this balance of physical positioning and reward, he will learn the action that corresponds to the word.

Please note that if you expect a dog to react to a command, he should be given fair warning. A command should always precede any action that you will perform in tandem with your dog. In other words, your dog deserves to be warned about what you want him to do next. He may be very clever but he cannot read your mind. For example, if you have him at heel and expect him to sit when you stop, say, 'Sit,' just before you come to a halt. In this way the dog will have time to register what you expect him to do and will act so that he ends up sitting in the correct position next to you. If you do not say the command until the moment of stopping, the dog cannot help but be out in front of you before he stops. In time, with careful, consistent training, he will learn to 'read' your body language and will be able to tell when you are about to stop and will sit at the right moment.

Dogs are extremely sensitive to the faintest changes in body language. My first Labrador, Christy, learnt to count and do simple arithmetic, and would bark the answers. It was a good party trick, but no one could tell how she did it and at first I did not know either. However, when she reached the correct number, without realizing it, I would relax my shoulders by an almost imperceptible amount. But she could perceive it and would stop barking.

If you accept that each command has a specific meaning as regards physical position and positioning, then if the dog does not assume or remain in that position, your response must be to tell him he is wrong. For example, if your dog understands the 'Sit' command and you tell him to sit but he remains standing, that is not 'Sit'. Therefore you should say 'No' or other scold words or sounds, and correct him physically. If you just repeat the command, three things can happen.

First, the dog begins counting how many times you will repeat the command. The domestic dog does not have a great many things to fill his day. He doesn't have to do tax returns, or make sure the washing comes in off the line before it rains, or remember to switch on the outside light for visitors. He doesn't have to worry about where his next meal is coming from or where he will sleep tonight. So he spends quite a lot of his waking hours trying to find ways to gain our attention. If he can make you say something to him more than once, he soon realizes that he receives correspondingly more attention if he refuses to obey than if he acted on your first command. The fact that it is disagreeable attention, because you are becoming more and more irritated, matters little to him. Words do not hurt.

Second, he may actually begin to believe that, for instance, the standing position is the 'Sit' because you keep saying 'Sit' while he is standing. It doesn't matter to him that you are saying 'Sit' more and more crossly: he will still think standing is 'Sit'. Eventually, when you are really cross, he may try the sit position, but in all this you have empowered him – he is training you to give him your time and attention.

This brings me to the third thing. If you have not insisted on an immediate response to the command and have repeated it until you are angry, you will not be able to bring yourself to say 'Good dog' when he does respond. This is very counterproductive.

The same is true of all your commands. If you repeat 'Come' when the dog is running away, he will think that that is what the command means, and so on. You should only say a command once. If you are sure he heard and understood you and he does not respond, your next word should be 'No'.

CHOOSING YOUR OWN COMMANDS

In addition to the four key commands, there are several specialist commands related to the gundog; the ones I use appear in the next chapter. I give alternatives, but the first in each case is my preferred command. Each command has a specific meaning, and it is important to choose one word or phrase for each meaning, or to make up your own command, and stick to it. Whatever words you choose, make sure that they are clear and distinct and sound different from one another.

CHAPTER 8

TEACHING THE KEY COMMANDS

The dog trainer's motto: Be fair, firm, vigilant and consistent.

The largest part of training a gundog is the curbing or directing of his natural instincts so that we have control. Control means focus and obedience: 'focus' in a dog means that whatever you ask him to do, he is in tune with you and will co-operate with you; it means he is not distracted by other things, dogs or people nearby. Obedience gives you a dog which is steady and responsive to his handler. A steady dog remains where the handler tells him, either sitting or walking to heel. A responsive dog acts in harmony with all his handler's commands and signals. If your dog is focused on you, you will have a team-mate who provides you with the pleasure of companionship in the field, and who is a valuable extension to your abilities.

A dog which is steady, focused and under control is energy efficient. He does not waste his own energy charging about aimlessly, and he does not waste yours through disobedience and trying your patience.

The 'Sit' signal, side view. The flat hand is raised no higher than the handler's forehead.

Teaching your Labrador the following commands will help you to achieve this happy sporting partnership.

THE SIT

The Command

'Sit' is the word most commonly used for retrievers, but sometimes the word 'Hup' is used. This derives

The 'Sit' signal, from behind the handler. The hand and face appear to the dog as two blobs, side by side.

from the days of muzzle-loading guns when the dog was expected to sit patiently while the gun was reloaded; the phrase 'Muzzles up' was used, and this became shortened to 'Hup', although 'Hup' is more commonly used with spaniels than with retrievers.

The 'Sit', or 'Stop' as it is also known, is the keystone to a gundog's training. He needs to understand and obey this command instantly in the field so that he can be considered absolutely under control, and also so he can be directed to the area where he should hunt for the retrieve.

The Hand Signal

The flat hand is raised no higher than the forehead, with the fingers always pointing skywards.

The Whistle Signal

The whistle signal is usually one short toot. You may prefer to give a medium or long toot instead, but whatever you choose, stick to it.

Definition

A dog should sit and remain sitting on voice command, whistle or hand signal, and should do so at any distance or angle from the handler. He must understand that when he has been told to sit, he must resist all temptations: these might include such things as a thrown dummy or ball, other dogs running about, and fur or feather suddenly appearing. Later he must learn that he should stop at any time when the instinct to chase is triggered.

The 'Sit' signal, given when the dog is seated beside the handler. The dog still sees two blobs, the face and the hand, side by side.

True steadiness could be described as a kind of self-discipline the dog learns, which causes him to sit or stop in response to a stimulus that would normally engender the instinct to chase. Another term for this might be 'conditioned reflex'. For example, he has set off for a retrieve and a pheasant starts up. He should sit or at least stop and watch it away or mark it if it is shot. He must not chase. He should then take directions to continue on his original quest, or indeed, to go for the newly shot bird if signalled to do so. All this is encompassed by the word 'steadiness'.

How To Do It

You may well have already taught your youngster to sit for his food, which will be a head start for you both. For one thing he will be facing you, and that is what we will want eventually, but at greater and greater distances.

We will want him to stop and look at us when we want him to change direction.

You should start with the dog on the lead at your side, the side on which you will walk him at heel. Have the lead in the hand away from the dog. Say the word 'Sit' in a pleasant voice, and lift his head with the lead while pushing down firmly but not roughly on his rump with your near hand. Be sure you push down on his rump and not on the middle of his back: in this way you will avoid causing any damage to his spine, and you will also be able to prevent his body swinging away from you. Alternatively, you can put the hand which is nearest to the dog under his rump in the crook of his hind leg and scoop him into a sitting position. When the dog is in the 'Sit' position, hold him there, praising him lavishly and repeating the word 'Sit' over and over.

Repeat this in the same way four or five times, then try just saying 'Sit', but moving your hands as if you were going to physically position him. Your lead hand, when it is raised, can soon be turned into the hand signal, which should be a flat hand, fingers pointing to the sky. The hand should not be raised higher than your forehead or it can easily be confused with the 'Get on' signal, which we will be discussing later. At a distance, your 'Sit' signal will appear as two blobs, side by side: your face and your hand. When your dog sees your raised hand, he should assume the 'Sit' position. If he does not, say 'No' firmly and physically position him, praise him, and let that do for that session. Put the dog away in his quiet place for the lesson to gel.

In the next training session, start as if you had not done the exercise before. After physically putting him into the 'Sit' position twice, try again without touching him, but with the hand movements. He should respond, but if he does not, go back to putting your hands on him, praising him and putting him away again. A titbit may help tremendously to expedite matters. Do not despise this, because the more quickly a dog learns something, the better and longer he will retain it.

There needs to be a good gap between training sessions, and I would probably not do more than two sessions in a day. Each session should only last for six minutes.

Quite soon, begin to follow your verbal command with your whistle signal – it is important to decide what this will be before you start to use it. I use a very short, sharp toot, much like the word 'Sit' in length, and I stop the toot with my tongue. Some people find this difficult so an 'open-ended' toot must do, or you can blow a longer toot if you wish.

Whatever you choose, make sure that you are consistent. If the toot is 'this long', keep it that long. More is not better, it is just different, and if it is different, the dog will not recognize it. It would not be fair of you to think that the dog is disobeying you if you have given him a signal that is different to the one you taught him.

Because dogs learn in pictures, you will have to teach him the 'Sit' at gradually increasing distances. He will not be able to understand at first that sitting should be done at a distance from you – he thinks of it as a geographical position in relation to you, not just a physical position.

I begin teaching this aspect of the stop whistle on the lead. I encourage the dog to move away from the heel position by using the release command. When he is at lead's length I say 'Sit', and blow the stop whistle signal, at the same time restraining him from moving by using the lead. He will try to come close to me, either to the heel position or to face me at my feet, because he thinks that is where 'Sit' is. I am trying to teach him that 'Sit' and the stop whistle mean 'Sit' wherever he is when he hears it, so if he continues to move after hearing me I will say 'No', and go to him, and gently but firmly put him on the spot where he was when he heard the whistle and my command.

As soon as he sits, I praise him sincerely, saying 'Sit', and blow the whistle a few times, distinctly but not loudly. Although the length of the toot must be consistent, the decibels should be reduced when you are near the dog. You must not deafen him. I then move back to where I was standing when I first gave the command, praising and repeating the command and the toot over and over again.

I repeat the exercise several times, each time asking him to sit at a different angle and distance from me so that eventually he connects the word not only with his physical position, but with its place in relation to me. When I think he has understood this, I try the same thing off the lead but at the same distance. If at any point he refuses to sit I will say 'No', and if he does

The 'Sit' signal from another angle. Note that the hand is flat and the fingers always point skywards.

sit, I will be so, so pleased. If things do not go well off lead, I will go back to doing the exercise with the lead attached. After a few successful efforts, I will put the dog away for his quiet time.

The next time I have him out training, when we reach the stop whistle part of the session, I will repeat as in the previous paragraph for a few times, then begin, little by little, to extend the distance. As I do this, I will produce something from my pocket immediately his bottom touches the ground. It might be a biscuit, a tennis ball, a glove or a small dummy. What I am trying to make him understand is that there is a point to him sitting to the command and to the whistle – and the point is, that I am going to show him something interesting. It is also important to keep up the praise at the same time. Also, if you do not show the dog some-

thing, you will eventually have him sitting as a pure discipline, but he will not necessarily look at you – and this defeats the object.

That stop whistle must come to mean a number of things. It means, 'Stop and look at me; I am going to show you something interesting, or maybe a signal, something to help you to achieve your goal.' For the Labrador, the goal is the retrieve. A dog can understand all this: one word or one toot can mean a collection of things. Next you should begin putting the toot before the word so that soon the two things are interchangeable. Eventually, the toot is what the dog knows at a distance and the verbal command is used at close quarters.

He must learn that 'Sit' means he has to remain sitting until you tell him to do something else. He should think that 'Sit' means 'Sit until next Tuesday; sit until I starve to death!' Teaching this should be done in very small steps. First, you make the dog sit still while you stand by him. Do not allow him to move for perhaps a minute. Next, take only one step away from him but to the side, always looking at him. Keeping your signal hand up will help. Gradually you move further away, always watching, praising and repeating the word 'Sit' while he remains still, checking with the lead and a 'No' if he shifts even slightly.

Often a young dog will move as you leave him. This may be because he wants to be with you, or he may want to be somewhere else; but it is most likely that he does not have the confidence that you will return to him. Some dogs are quite anxious about remaining still while you go away, and will not allow you to go at all when they are off lead. With this type of dog, it can be very effective to tie his lead to a fence giving him about a yard of slack. Then, facing him and standing very close to him, say your command, give the sit signal and praise him quietly. Then just put one foot behind you, rock on to it and then back towards the dog again. This should go well and if so, step away with both feet, then towards him again. Don't be tempted to go further or for longer just because he is tethered: you are trying to build his confidence, trying to make the experience pleasurable. In time, in this slow, baby step way, you will be able to go further and further for longer and longer. When you try it with the lead off, you will need to go back to the beginning of little by little. Remember, you can build on success but not on failure.

When you have been successful in leaving a dog for the length of time you feel right, return to him with your chin up or your face turned slightly away. You will still be able to see him but you are not being confrontational. If you go back to him looking at him full-face, he will assume he has done something wrong and will almost certainly move. After all, whenever he moved in the past, you returned to replace him on his spot and you looked straight at him and probably scolded him. If he is where he should be, you must appear unthreatening as you walk back to him.

Be sure to note where you left him because he knows the spot exactly. If you put him on another spot he will view this as 'getting away with it'. The same rule applies when you blow the stop whistle. Note where he was when you blew the whistle and if he bounds on, go out to him and take him back to the exact buttercup or daisy that he should be sitting on. You can be niggly with him while you are returning him to the spot, but once he is there, you must be nice to him. It is where you want him to be, after all, and you want him to want to be there.

Every time you change anything in the process of teaching an exercise, you may well have to take the rest of the exercise back to basics. For instance, if you move to another field to train, you should treat the dog as if he has not had the lesson before, because as he sees it, he never has had the lesson before – not *there* anyway – and he does not think the command applies: 'I've never heard that word here before. It can't mean the same thing.' Similarly, after working on the lead, he will not realize that the same words mean the same thing when you remove the lead. Go back to the beginning.

This all sounds quite repetitive and time-consuming, but we are teaching the dog what is to him a foreign language; we are teaching him things which go against his instincts. It does take time and there are no shortcuts. When you feel like hurrying things up, remember that you are training, not testing.

Eventually the dog will realize that each command means the same thing wherever he is – not just at home, but in the field next door, the hill a mile away, the woods beyond the hill, in Dorset, Cumbria, Scotland.

THE RECALL

The Command

The command for the recall is 'Come' ('Come here', or 'Here').

The Hand Signal

Pat the front of your thigh. With a young dog, raise both hands out to your side in a welcome while you lean forwards. However, as time goes by, use this posture less and less. It is very effective with a young dog, but you would not do it if you had a gun in your hand.

The Whistle Signal

The whistle signal for the recall is either two short pips, repeated like the beat of a galloping horse's feet, or three or more short, sharp pips. Keep to whichever you choose.

Definition

The recall may be defined as follows: 'Come right up to me', or 'Come closer to me'.

In the initial stages 'Come' should mean 'Come right up to me'. It is important that when the dog does return to you, you put your hand on his head; this policy will help you to achieve a good delivery at the end of a retrieve.

Later on, your command and whistle signal may sometimes mean that you only want the dog to come in closer to you. This might be when the retrieve is closer to you than he is.

How To Do It

A dog that will come will bring, so the recall is integral to the retrieve. Just as the sit and the retrieve are taught together, the recall must also be part of the picture. A dog that will not come on command will not bring the retrieve.

As with the training of the sit and heelwork, you should begin with the dog on the lead – a lead of about six feet is good. Sit him, and back away to the extent of the lead. Give him your recall command and bend forwards: this will draw him towards you. Dogs are instinctively drawn to things which are diminishing in size – I suppose this is because any prey they might chase appears to become smaller as it runs away. As he starts towards you, tell him 'Good dog', and reel him gently up to you. Make sure you get your hands on his head, and fondle his ears while you praise and repeat your recall command. You should do this because eventually you want him to bring the dummy right up to you and present it in a face-to-face position. Later, when he brings you a retrieve, you should put your hand on his head before taking the article.

After you have praised him for the recall, and not before, tell him to sit, then praise him for that. Putting him in the sit is what you will do once the dog has delivered a retrieve, and it gives you control by preventing him from going off and perhaps getting into trouble.

As with other commands, you should do this exercise first on the lead, then off the lead but at the same distance. Gradually increase the distance you go from the dog before calling him.

But now you must take care because the dog will begin to anticipate what you want and will come before you call. He must not think you will always call him, so be sure to go back to him two times out of three, just to keep him guessing. In any case, you will hardly ever have to call your dog to you from the sitting position in the shooting field; it is far more likely that he will be showing you his backside, galloping away, just when you want him to return to you.

So you need to teach him to come when he is moving away from you. Have him on the lead and give your release command. When he is at lead's length from you, call him. If he does not start to come, give a tug on the lead and say 'No'. However, if he does show the smallest sign of responding to your call, he should be encouraged and praised.

I have found that different dogs react differently to their handlers when performing the recall. Some dogs love to be praised from the moment of their first response to the handler's call and are encouraged to speed up their return; others take the praise to mean that they have done all that is required, so they veer off and begin to suit themselves. The remedy for the latter type of dog is to withhold your praise until he reaches you, then to be really effusive. Remember to put your hands on the dog's head when he comes up to you.

Another important variation to work at is to get your dog to come when you have your back to him. Proceed as follows: sit him and walk away. When you are about ten paces from him, blow your recall whistle, but keep walking. Look over your shoulder: it is usual to find that the dog has not moved. This is partly because you are not presenting the usual picture to him, and partly because the whistle sounds different.

Do the following experiment: ask a friend to blow the whistle, first while facing you and again when turned

The recall. Always make a point in the early days that the dog comes right up to you and that you touch him on the head. This causes him to raise his head – dogs turn towards touch – and this will help you to achieve a good delivery in due course.

away from you. You may be surprised to hear how different it sounds. So to get your dog moving towards you, you will have to encourage him by half turning, clapping your hands, using your voice and bending down – but all the while keep on walking, and repeat the whistle signal when your back is to him. Eventually your dog will realize that although the whistle sounds different, and you look different, it all means the same thing: he must come.

This exercise is useful in the move towards the situation where he is out of sight of you, perhaps in a wood or with his back to you, but he must still recognize the recall whistle and respond. The same is true of the stop whistle.

HEELWORK

The Command

The most usual command is 'Heel' (or 'Close' or 'Walk').

The Hand Signal

When walking forwards with the dog, pat the front of your thigh, the one nearest him. If you pat the side of your thigh, it tends to make the dog hang back to look at your hand.

When the dog is being called into heel from another position, another signal is required. If he is facing you, or is away to the side, use your hand with a pointing finger and circling action to indicate the path he should take in order to arrive at the heel position.

There is no whistle signal for this command.

Definition

'Heel' is the position a dog should assume and maintain at his handler's side (always one side), facing forward with his handler, his head or shoulder level with the handler's knee, stationary or walking. He should not surge ahead, lag behind, sniff the ground or widen the gap to the side. He should keep pace with his handler and be focused on him, ready for changes in speed or direction. We like a dog to be in this position so that, with our height, we can see things before he does – for example, a rabbit or deer in the next field. Another reason is that, although we can see him, he will not be in the way if we have to turn towards him.

Good heelwork should begin when a puppy has his

*Heelwork. Correct signal –
pat the front of your thigh
to encourage your dog to
come into and maintain
the correct heel position.*

*Heelwork. Incorrect signal
– patting the side of your
thigh will make your dog
hang back as he will be
anxious that his nose
will be in the way of your
hand.*

first collar and lead. He should never be allowed to pull on or chew it. Obviously you must be very gentle with a youngster, but you can still make it nicer for him to walk on a slack lead than to pull.

If heelwork is not taught correctly in the early train-

ing of your young dog, poor performance will plague you for the whole of his life. The only remedy for poor heelwork is to change your command and start afresh, making the new word mean absolutely what it should.

The following tale illustrates this. I was competing

with my fox-red Labrador bitch, Coral, in an Open trial at Windsor some years ago. She was one of the best dogs I have ever had – kind, intelligent, good-looking, usually obedient and a great gamefinder. But her heelwork was not her best point. We were walking up in white grass and she was moving a few inches ahead of me over every few yards. When I could, I whispered, 'Heel!' and she would correct herself – but not for long. Presently she was a yard in front. Then a shot was fired and she leapt forwards another yard. The judge told me to put my lead on – and there we were, on the long trek home without having picked a single bird.

I was mortified, and what made it worse was that I had been drawn to run her in another trial at Holkham in a week's time. So this is what I did. I resolved never to use the word 'Heel' to her again, but used a new word, 'Close,' meaning just what I have described in the definition above. I was determined and meticulous over this re-training, and heelwork was never a problem again. We did not win at Holkham – she failed to find a hare in roots – but her heelwork was impeccable.

How To Do It

I feel that it is important to teach the basic commands on the lead. In this way you have the dog under your physical control, and can immediately prevent things going wrong, or correct them when they do go wrong. Thus you quickly come to the point where you can praise the dog, which is every bit as important as correcting him. You must assess your dog's temperament as early as you can. You need to be much gentler with a soft, responsive dog than with a tough, resistant dog.

Decide which side suits you best. Right-handed Guns will carry their gun on their right arm so they will prefer the dog to be on the left so that the gun barrels do not knock him on the head. Left-handed Guns will prefer the dog to be on their right. What follows is the way for a right-handed person to train a dog to walk to heel on the left. If you wish your dog to walk on your right, you can just reverse the method to suit you.

Because our ultimate aim is to work the dog free of the lead, and because dogs learn in pictures, we need

to remember that what he sees is really important to him. When your dog has been trained to walk to heel, with no collar and no lead, when he is naked, he will see you walking upright, looking ahead, with both arms relaxed. He will see the hand which is nearest him hanging relaxed and empty by his face. Try to give this impression from the beginning. Take the lead in your right hand, your strong hand, so it comes across your body from the dog. Your left hand hangs loosely near his face. If you need extra strength to give the lead a more effective or positioning jerk, you can always add the left hand, but make sure to release that hold when you release the tension. Most of the time the left hand should be free to encourage, pat or position the dog, or indeed, to give him a titbit.

Sit the dog beside you with his shoulder level with your leg, both of you looking in the same direction. Relax your right elbow and have the lead quite loose; there should be no tension in it. Dogs turn towards touch so when you are about to move off, lean down and just gently brush the back of your hand against the cheek and side of his muzzle nearest you, say 'Heel' and move forwards. You can use this gentle touch against his cheek often during training to keep his attention. Do not reach across and touch the far side of his face; this will cause him to turn away from you. You should say 'Heel' before you move so the dog can register the command and be ready to accompany you.

As soon as you start to walk forwards, your dog will almost certainly begin to move ahead of you. You must correct him immediately. In the case of heelwork, it is important not to allow the dog to leave the heel position by more than an inch or two before stopping him. It is important not to get into what I call 'the yoyo situation', where the dog is allowed to forge out in front of the handler to the full extent of the lead. He then usually throws his whole weight into the lead and pulls like a carthorse. Only then does the handler pull him back into position, and while he pulls back on the lead he says 'Heel!' in a cross voice. Then he allows the dog to repeat the process again almost immediately.

This gives the dog a confused message. He should think that 'Heel' means the position described in the definition above, but hearing it in the wrong position, he can easily come to believe that anywhere could be

'Heel'. The dog should only hear the command when you first call him into position, and after that, only when he is in the correct position. He should not think that it means any other position. Saying 'Heel' even very crossly, is still saying 'Heel.'

So we have two points here. First, you must not let the dog move more than a couple of inches out of the right position before correcting him; and second, you must say 'No!' sharply, but not loudly, as you correct him. When he is back in the heel position, you can say 'Heel' in a normal voice to make him realize that that is where 'Heel' is. Imagine that when the dog is in the correct position, he is inside an oblong box beside you. This is his comfort zone. In this box he is a good dog, a comfortable dog, and you are pleased with him. Outside the box, even one inch outside, is not 'Heel', it is 'No!' He is not comfortable, you are not pleased.

Why does a dog pull on the lead? There are several reasons. First, it does not hurt the dog. Over the thousands of generations of dogs, the neck area has been used by the more dominant dogs to grasp and punish pack members who have not shown the right amount of submissiveness. Also, young dogs and puppies hang onto each others' scruffs and cheeks in play. Because of this, the skin of the neck and cheeks has become very insensitive; it is very thinly endowed with nerve endings. So it does not hurt a dog to pull on the lead. However, it is not natural for the neck and windpipe to take this pressure and it certainly cannot be good for the dog. It is anathema to me to hear that ghastly rasping sound of a dog on a tight lead.

Another reason dogs pull is to be in front, to be the leader. They pull because they can, and they pull because they do not realize that they have a choice. We need to demonstrate to the dog that he has a choice. He can be in the right position and be comfortable and receive praise, or he can be wrong and very uncomfortable. We want him to choose to be the good dog, the dog which knows what 'Heel' means, the dog which is praised.

When you have to correct the dog, say 'No!' sharply and jerk the lead smartly out to your right. This is not a positioning movement, it is a disciplinary action. It is not simultaneous either; it is consecutive. Say 'No!' just a fraction of a second before you apply the jerk. The

Heelwork. This dog is just a bit wide of the handler – a bit outside the 'box' that constitutes the correct 'Heel' position. He is focused on the handler, however, so a 'No' in a moderate voice should make him correct himself without needing to be tugged on the lead.

word is a warning of the discomfort to come, and soon your dog should respond to 'No' and correct himself without you having to apply the jerk. Do not nag him with little pulls on the lead; he will not mind, and you will never have a dog which is reliable at heel. You must impress the dog with your jerk. You should want to get the unpleasant part of this over and done with as soon as possible. Your dog should say to himself, 'This is pretty horrid, I don't want it to keep happening. If I hear my handler say "No!" again, I'll know what's coming, I will correct myself!' If you have allowed the dog to get out in front of you, you will have to add your left hand to the lead in order to bring him back into place. Once the dog is back in the heel position, say the word 'Heel' and praise him lavishly. Only through this balance of correction and praise will the dog learn the meaning of the command properly.

Your dog should never be allowed to pull on the lead, neither should he chew or lunge suddenly on it. It is not his lead, it is yours. He did not go down to the pet shop and buy it, you did. It is your property, not his, and he has no business pulling on it, so do not let him get away with it. When you feel him begin to put tension into the lead, say 'No' and give the lead a tug. Bring him back into a comfortable position, and praise him. You will have to be very determined about this, more determined than he is.

If he has the lead in his mouth, you must not jerk it or you could damage his teeth. In this case you must say 'No!' sharply, and if he does not release his hold, give him a firm slap on the muzzle, one that he will not want repeated; then immediately praise him when he has let go.

It bears repeating that you must, of course, know what kind of dog you have: thus you would be much gentler with a sensitive, compliant dog than with a brash, insubordinate type of dog. Using a check chain, whatever your dog's temperament, will be kinder than a rope lead as the noise it makes warns the dog of the discomfort to come. The chain also loosens more readily than a rope lead does.

The transition from on the lead to off the lead is best done gradually. With the check chain and soft lead, this is made easier than with a rope slip lead. When your dog will walk nicely beside you on a slack lead, you are ready to try the next step. Walk along with the dog at heel, and after a few paces, still continuing to walk, reach down and, as surreptitiously as possible, undo the clip from the collar, at the same moment saying 'Heel'. Brush his cheek with the back of your hand. Continue for five paces only and then say 'Sit', and stop. By walking for just five paces you will feel in control, and you will be in a position to praise your

dog. If you go further, you stand the chance of losing his concentration and then you will have to correct him.

After three or four successful short stints, you can try to do an extra pace or two. Presently you will be able to walk comfortably for several yards, but if at any time the dog leaves the correct position, clip the lead back on to the collar and go back a stage.

When you feel the time is right, you can begin to make the transition to having both collar and lead off. Take the chain from around the dog's neck. Do this while you are stationary. Let the chain run out to its full length, then clip the lead on to one ring. Loop the chain under your dog's neck from your side, and up and over his neck on the far side so that it is draped around and over the neck. Say 'Heel', touch his face, and start forwards – but for just five paces. If all goes well, as you begin to walk again, slowly shorten the lead so that the chain slides off and ends up hanging alongside his neck, just touching him. You are slowly accustoming him to losing the feel of physical contact with you. If at any point you begin to lose his attention, put him back on the collar and lead.

You will know when it is time to try the next step. Reassemble the chain into its loop and clip the lead on to both rings. Hold the lead so the collar dangles beside the dog's neck. The touch of the chain will remind him of what he should do. It's almost like stepping stones: you are easing him away from being on lead to being off lead, little by little. Soon he will be ready for you to move the lead quietly into the hand away from him so that he is completely naked, untouched, but still at heel.

Often, when you start off lead work, your dog will leave the side you have been training him on and try to walk on the other side of you. This is because he has been corrected on the primary side, and feels that if he changes sides, he will not be corrected. However, you must not let him think this: he must not think he can choose. Be consistent: speak sharply to him immediately he moves to the wrong side, and swing the lead into his face or give him a light tap on the muzzle. In the next moment, bend your body to the side he should be on, and encourage him to return to that side with kind words and a kind hand and perhaps a treat. If this fails, you will need to put the lead back on and refresh his memory. Use lots of praise and perhaps a treat when he is in the correct position. Make it preferable to be right.

Heelwork practice is probably one of the more tedious parts of training your Labrador, but it is a vital component of the finished article. If ever you see dogs doing heelwork to music, you will realize that they obviously derive huge pleasure from doing it well. We should be able to make heelwork enjoyable for our Labradors, too. Be enthusiastic and show your dog how pleased you are with good work, and give him a treat occasionally. If you can do a little good heelwork every day, preferably in different places, you will make good progress.

'Heel' means 'Come into the correct heel position', as well as 'Maintain the heel position'. In other words, if your dog is away to one side of you, behind you, or facing you, you should be able to say 'Heel', and he will move himself into position. With practice, this can come to look a little like heelwork to music and can be amusing to you and your dog. Its practical application is to get the dog moving, without being touched, into a position where he is lined up with you to go in the right direction for the retrieve. It can also be used when you are walking and the dog is running free. You may see a flock of sheep ahead so you will want the dog to come in to the heel position to pass them.

Start with the dog sitting beside you, say the command 'Sit', and put up your hand signal for the sit. (This is the raised flat right hand, and you will be bringing your hand across your body from right to left so that your palm faces the dog at about shoulder height.) Carefully walk forwards to the end of the lead, keeping your back to the dog, but watching to be sure he does not move. Say 'Heel', and pat the front of your thigh with your left hand and draw him up alongside you with the lead. Sit him when he reaches your side.

Next, leave him sitting as before, but as you ask him to come towards you, start to walk forwards, encouraging him to come into the heel position and walk along with you for a few paces. Next, try it off the lead. If successful, gradually increase the distance you go before you call him and the distance you walk with him at heel before stopping. If unsuccessful, put the lead back on and begin again. When all is going well,

you can change things bit by bit. You can free him with your release command, and when he is not too far from you, call him in to heel while you are walking.

Occasionally when a dog is called in to heel from behind, he will shoot past his handler. Be ready for this. Keep your eye on him, and when he is one or two bounds from joining you, repeat your heel command and use your hands to encourage him to slow down and assume the correct position at your side.

To get the dog to come in to the heel position from the front, have him sit beside you. Then move so that you are facing him. He should be on the lead and the lead should be in your left hand. Say 'Heel', step backwards with your left foot, and at the same time draw him towards your left side with the lead. Your movement back starts him moving; your hand on the lead reinforces the motion and will become the signal. As he comes beside you, step forwards again, encouraging him with your hands and voice. He should turn inwards and finish up at heel. You then say 'Sit'. If you tell him to sit at just the right moment, he should end up in exactly the right position. Practice makes perfect. Please note that your right foot does not move during this exercise.

After a few repetitions you should be able to dispense with the lead, and get him to move to your side with the command and your foot and hand movements only. Finally, just moving your hand with a pointing finger in an anti-clockwise way will bring him in to heel. A treat can greatly speed up this exercise.

STEADINESS

Technically, steadiness is not a command, but an essential that goes hand in hand with the sit, the recall and heelwork, and needs no extra command. Steadiness is built into the training of these three key commands.

Once your dog has learnt the commands 'Sit', 'Come' and 'Heel', you can begin to expand his understanding of being steady. Steadiness means that he has to remain at heel or in the sit position, or come to you immediately the moment he is called, even when sorely tempted to do otherwise. The prime temptations for your Labrador would be the retrieve and other moving objects – for example, another dog running about, or rabbits, birds and cats. Other distractions would include his handler

Steadiness training. With your dog sitting, stand approximately a metre from him and to one side. Have the lead in the hand nearest the dog but without any tension in it. It is vital that you watch your dog at all times. Have a dummy in your free hand and show it to the dog. When his attention is on it, place the dummy on the ground but do not allow the dog to move. If he does, check him firmly with the lead. Try not to say 'No' – you don't want him to think 'Never'. After the tug on the lead, say 'Sit'. Pick up the dummy by hand without taking your eyes off him, repeating the word 'Sit' about every two seconds and praising him intermittently.

or other people pointing at something, waving to each other, or suddenly moving about near him.

When your dog is truly steady, you will be able to point in the direction of a falling bird and say 'Mark', and he will know he is to look where you point, but not to go. You will be able to clap your hands or have a conversation with a friend, and he will not go. Perhaps most importantly, you will be able to work a second dog and the first will sit staunchly and patiently.

Your dog should come to believe that you have eyes in the back of your head. Once he is sitting, turn your face away but keep your eye on him. When you do any dummy throwing, do the same thing. If you shoot, have your dog with you when you are practising mounting your gun. Mount the gun frequently with your face averted from your dog but always keeping an eye on him. If he looks in the least bit like breaking the sit command, or heel or the recall, you will be in a position to respond quickly.

If your dog enjoys carrying things about and will come reliably when you call, then you can start using the retrieve to teach him steadiness. If he is not keen on dummies or is unwilling to carry things about, you will need to find something that does interest him, perhaps

Steadiness training. If and when the dog is steady to the placed dummy, you can toss it gently, but always watch the dog to be sure he does not run-in. Keep saying, 'Sit.'

LEFT: Steadiness training. The dog remains steady to the gently thrown dummy but he is very interested.

BELOW: Steadiness training. This is wrong because the handler has taken her eyes off the dog. Luckily, the dog seems to be steady.

a toy or a knuckle bone. If he is not reliable on the recall, you should not use the retrieve for steadiness training until he is.

With a dog who will come to call and who is interested in dummies, you can proceed with the following exercise. The whole exercise should be carried out in a very calm, controlled and unexciting way. Put the check chain and lead on the dog and sit him down at heel. Show him a dummy, then move away to the side so that you are standing at a right angle to him, holding the end of the lead in your left hand, the hand nearest him, with just the slightest tension in it – what a horseman would call 'a feel on the rein'. In this position, you will be able to see the smallest flex of a muscle, and any intention to run-in. You will be able to check him using the lead, or, if he is too quick for you, it will be possible for you to intercept him as he runs-in.

Have the dummy in your right hand, the hand away from the dog, and show it to him again, saying 'Sit' clearly, but not loudly. Let him see you place the dummy on the ground a couple of feet from you on the side away from him. The dummy should always be close enough for you to reach it without having to tighten the lead. In this position, you will be able to intercept the dog if he darts towards the dummy. It is most important that you watch him all the time so that you can see the slightest sign that he wants to go. Do your utmost to prevent him moving from the sit. Keep repeating the sit command over and over.

You should try your best not to say 'No' during this exercise, as you are going to show the dog a moving dummy several times which he is not to go for, and you do not want him to think 'Never'. Just keep saying 'Sit', and praise him as much as you can along with your command. I say something like 'Sit, good dog, sit, sit, good dog, sit,' so I am interspersing my praise with the command. If he moves, even a little, you must check him with the lead and return him to the sit. As you replace him on his spot, say 'Sit' nicely, and run your hand over the top of his head. Keep the 'upper hand' and do not fondle him below eye level.

If he is particularly excited or overwrought, the muzzle-holding technique may do wonders to calm him. When he is settled, pick up the dummy. You can do this without taking your eyes off him because you can see the dummy in your peripheral vision. Keep praising him along with your 'Sit' command.

Next, drop the dummy from about waist height as quietly as you can so that it lands in much the same place as before. Dropping it is slightly more exciting than simply placing it. Keep calmly repeating 'Sit'. If all is going well, you can then toss the dummy very slightly, though it should still land next to you and be close enough for you to pick up without tightening the lead. Go back to the dog from time to time and praise him for being still.

You can see by now that we are building the idea in the dog's mind that 'Sit' means that he must remain still, despite temptation, and he will be praised. However, 'Sit' also means that something interesting is about to happen. You can see, too, that we are achieving steadiness in very tiny steps, and this is the best and surest way to teach a dog anything new. Mighty oaks from tiny acorns grow.

Eventually you will see that the dog is steady enough for you to place, drop and toss the dummy at the same distance from him, but without the lead in your hand. Have the lead on, but lying on the ground beside him outside his field of vision; if he moves, you can take hold of it quickly and return him to his place. You can be a little stern with him because he has moved, but you must be nice to him once he is sitting on his spot again. Go back to holding the lead until you feel sure he has the right idea.

Once you feel he really understands that he must not move, the next step is to repeat the whole performance with the lead wrapped round his neck, or indeed detached from the collar. When you take the lead off, put it in your pocket so your hands are free. Go through the whole business of placing, dropping and tossing the dummy while standing as you did at the beginning. When you feel you have the focus you are looking for – in other words, that he is intent on what you want, and accepts that he must remain still – you can move away a little and repeat the same actions with the dummy as before. Again, we are taking only baby steps.

'Reading' the dog is vital here. He may be a calm, phlegmatic type; he may be excitable and hyper-active. The more excitable the dog, the calmer and slower you need to be. This is not a race against time: it is an investment for the future, an investment of your time.

The picture the dog sees is very important to him, so begin to change things little by little until you can actually throw the dummy a short distance and pick it up yourself. Presently you will be able to move, say, twenty metres from the dog and throw the dummy a few metres. At this point you may feel that you can leave the dummy and walk back to the dog: do so carefully, always being sure that you could intercept him if he starts to run-in.

If he has remained in place by the time you reach him, move to his side, say his name, and slowly and carefully give him the hand signal known as the 'chop' signal, which is described in the next section. The 'chop' signal will later be used for the unseen retrieve, together with the command to retrieve. I sometimes find that the dog is hesitant at this point because I have been concentrating for so long on keeping him still, but with encouragement and a conspiratorial tone, he will usually set off for the dummy.

Your dog must also learn to be steady to temptation when he is walking at heel. Many trainers use a shrill 'Brrrrrr' noise to herald the flight of a dummy through the air. Put the lead on your dog and start walking with him at heel. Have a dummy in your right hand. After a few paces, make the 'Brrrrrr' noise and say 'Sit'. As soon as he is sitting, throw the dummy or tennis ball a few yards in front of you. Use the lead to restrain him if necessary and keep repeating 'Sit'. After a short wait, say 'Heel', walk forward with the dog and pick up the article by hand. The dog must be prevented from touching it. Praise him as much as possible during this exercise and keep any scolding to a minimum. Usually, dogs understand very quickly that they must sit when they hear the 'Brrrrrr' – they like to sit because they think sitting makes the dummy go. On the third or fourth throw, you can probably very carefully remove the lead and send the dog with 'Hie lost' and the little chop signal.

Often, I find that when I have reached the point where I can do this exercise off the lead, the dog disappears from my heel. I look around and there he is, a few yards back, sitting, because he believes that sitting makes things fly through the air!

Steadiness training must include ensuring that your dog comes to you reliably in spite of distractions. First, of course, he must come reliably when there are no distractions and in several different places. He should come to voice and whistle. When you feel confident that he responds well, ask a friend to join you. Prime the friend to back you up by saying 'No!' when he hears you say 'No!', and when he hears you say 'Good dog' he should back you up in that, too. Let the dog go up to the other person, and after a few seconds, call the dog. If the dog does not obey, you must say 'No!', and the other person should say 'No!' too, and behave as if he is displeased with the dog, then when the dog turns to go to you he should praise him as you do. You do not want the dog to be afraid of him.

Next, ask the other person to have a dog with him. Let the dogs become acquainted and play a little, but on the lead. Next, walk your dog away about twenty paces and then free him, using your release command. He will probably bound up to the other dog whereupon you call or whistle him. If he turns and comes straightaway you should be delighted and tell him so, but if he ignores you, say 'No!' and your friend should back you up and say 'No!' too. When you see the smallest sign that he wants to comply with you, praise him and repeat your command.

You can see how you can use this exercise in different places and at varying distances with other friends who understand what you are trying to do. Change the circumstances and the picture the dog sees as many times as you can think of, but always insist on instant obedience. Make coming preferable to not coming.

Having made sure your Labrador is good in the presence of livestock (*see* Chapter 5, in the section 'Stock, Poultry and Cats'), you can improve and extend your dog's understanding of 'instant recall' by practising with distractions and temptations nearby. Practise in a field next to one where farm animals are grazing. At first it would be advisable to have a hedge between you and the stock, but later a wire fence will do. Leave the dog sitting while you walk away, and when you have gone ten paces, call or whistle the dog to come. Alternatively, allow him to run free to a distance of about ten paces, then call him. Introduce the reward of a tennis ball or dummy being thrown out towards him for him to retrieve when he is on his way to you. Alternatively, you can use an edible reward. This teaches him that it is worthwhile ignoring the stock and coming to command. Do not be rooted to the spot, move towards the dog if you have to reprimand him. Equally, be effusive with your praise if he gives a good response. You need to be the preferable option as opposed to that of his giving the other animals his attention.

CHAPTER 9

THE RETRIEVE

Most Labradors are keen to retrieve, and breeders of working Labradors have been honing this skill in their stock for many generations. The little test I spoke of in Chapter 1 can show how innate this instinct is. However, sometimes a puppy will show a strong wish to retrieve at five or six weeks, but then at about four months he seems to lose interest. Do not worry: the retrieving instinct will surface again, possibly as late as at nine or ten months. I have not heard of a Labrador that showed the instinct at five weeks that did not have it as an adult.

Once your dog has learnt steadiness and will watch dummies, balls and toys thrown, he is ready to move on to more advanced training. There are three basic types of retrieve. With each of these, the dog is sent from the heel position. For our purposes, the handler is right-handed and the dog is at heel on his left. The first type is a straightforward seen retrieve which involves no handling beyond sending the dog, using only his name, and receiving delivery. The second is a seen retrieve with a delay. The dog should be sent on his name but with a sweeping hand motion indicating the direction. The handler completes the exercise by taking delivery. The third is the unseen or blind retrieve of which the dog has no knowledge. The handler must use a special sending command, and he may need to give the dog other directions to guide him to the right area; he will need to take delivery on the dog's return. Each type of retrieve should be managed in a different way. The straightforward seen retrieve is described above. There is no signal or command for this. For the delayed seen retrieve, the casting hand should sweep close to and past the dog's face, indicating the direction of the retrieve. Remember to watch your dog to ensure that he is looking in the right direction before he

goes. The dog's name is spoken as your hand begins to move. No other command is necessary. For the third type of retrieve, the unseen, I recommend that when casting your dog out, your flat hand should be placed alongside and nearly touching the dog's muzzle, pointing in the direction you wish the dog to go. Before you give the command to go, you should have established in your mind the direction you mean him to go, then look at him so you know he is looking there. When you send him, say the command and give a short chop or flick with your hand. I prefer the chop. I believe very strongly that there must be some movement of the casting hand when the dog is allowed to go. There must be no uncertainty in his mind as to whether you want him to go or not. Your signals should never be vague or ambiguous: the dog should be given a clear indication so that there is no doubt in his mind about the direction he should follow. What a dog sees is more important to him than what he hears.

WORKING CONDITIONS

The Terrain

Choose ground that is rough but not too challenging. A meadow of mixed uncut grasses of between 4in and 24in in height would be ideal. A field as flat as a billiard table is not good because the retrieves will be too easy and the dog is liable to become too gleeful. He may pounce on the dummy, toss it into the air or lie down to chew it.

The Wind

The wind is very important to a dog. It carries scent

to his nostrils so that he can find the retrieve. He does not rely on sight as we do, and it is sometimes surprising to watch a dog working only a foot or two upwind of a dummy and still not be able to find it. This said, dogs do not like to work straight into the wind. This is, I think, because they know the chances of catching scent are restricted. Scent particles leave the retrieve article and spread out in a fan or cone downwind, gradually becoming more and more diffuse and therefore harder to catch. The strength of the wind is an important factor – the stronger it is, the more rapidly the scent molecules are scattered. If a dog is working straight into the wind, he will be lucky if he catches a number of scent molecules, enough to lead him to the fall. If he is working across the wind, he stands more chance of catching the molecules and finding where they are more concentrated and this will lead him in to find the retrieve. If he is working down the wind, he will catch part of the 'fan' after he has passed the article and will turn to try to catch more scent. If turning one way does not work, the other way should. However, dogs do have to learn to work into the wind. An experienced dog which is allowed to use his natural abilities will, when he catches the faintest hint of scent, traverse the wind back and forth in order to find the strongest concentration of scent molecules so that he can gradually 'home in' on the retrieve. This traversing is called quartering.

When training a young dog, you should try to make his chances of success as likely as you can, to keep him keen and interested. Therefore, work him downwind or across the wind to his seen retrieves. When you start on unseens, working him diagonally towards a very gentle but steady wind would be the right choice. Many things will affect the direction and strength of the wind. On flat ground it will be fairly predictable. To find its direction, turn your face until you can feel it blowing equally on both cheeks. When you can feel this, you will know that the wind is blowing straight towards your nose. In a wood, the wind will bounce off the trees and around shrubs and be somewhat diverted by them, but generally it will carry scent in a fairly consistent direction. Coming over a hedge, a wall or a heap of branches or brashings, it will roll over like a wave coming to a beach, and scent will be carried back in towards the base of the barrier or heap. On water, whether moving or still, which has high banks the wind can be very fluky and confusing to both dog and handler. Watching the leaves of trees or the way grass bends to the wind can tell you its direction. Other ways of ascertaining the wind direction include tossing a few strands of grass in the air or holding up a wet finger, but I do not find these two methods as accurate as the 'face test'.

The Sun

I do not think dogs see into the sun any better than we do, so it is worth bearing this in mind when choosing where to throw your dummies – that is to say, try to throw 'down sun' or across the path of sunlight for your young dog so he has the best chance of marking the fall. The day will come, however, when the retrieve does land 'up sun'. Sound helps a dog to pinpoint the fall almost as much as sight, and this can come in useful when the retrieve is unseen due to bright sunlight.

Dummies and Throwing Them

Because it is not always possible to obtain game for training, we use dummies instead. Even if we could find 'the real thing' all the year round, an animal or bird carcass would have limited use due to the fact that decomposition takes place sooner or later. In any case, when a carcass has been retrieved two or three times, it becomes wet with dog saliva and the corpse becomes very tempting to chew. To keep on throwing or even placing the same carcass over and over again will encourage a dog to view the object as a toy, and this is not a good idea.

Some dogs lose interest in dummies, but I believe that in most cases this is the fault of the trainer. My own dogs have all maintained an interest in dummies for the whole of their life, and these have been dogs of several different breeds and many different lines. I have therefore come to the conclusion that it must be the way I operate that keeps their interest, and I believe there are four main things I do, that ensure my dogs are always keen to retrieve dummies.

The first is that I make my dogs know that retrieving is a privilege, something they are allowed to do when I feel like it. It is not a duty or a right.

Secondly, the number of retrieves given in any one session is restricted according to the dog's level of interest. If he is not madly keen he has perhaps two or three retrieves in a session, and on some days he will have none at all. The fanatical dog makes faster progress. You can give him more retrieves per session and teach him more in the way of steadiness and hand signals, but make sure you always quit while he still wants more.

The third thing I make sure of is to use a number of different dummies; I seldom throw the same dummy twice in a training session. It's obvious really: if you continually throw the same dummy, the dog will think that you do not value it. Perhaps he even thinks, 'Every time I bring it back, he throws it away again. It can't be worth much so I think I'll play with it, run away with it, chew it and toss it in the air.' Although dummies can be the same colour, shape, weight and size, you can make them distinguishable by putting a different number on

the top end of each with an indelible felt-tip pen. When you put the dummies in your bag, make sure they sit up vertically so you can tell them all apart; if they lie horizontally, you may keep taking out the top one over and over again. Each time a dummy is thrown it acquires new smells according to where it lands and according to which dog brings it back. This makes each one different to a dog. People often ask me what a dummy smells of, and I reply that it smells of the material of which it is made, the thrower's hands, the game bag, and the places where it has landed. Thus it may smell of perhaps mud, grass or flowers, moss or cow dung, and of course dog saliva.

Lastly, I always make the dog know that I am very pleased indeed to have the dummy he has brought me. Particularly with a young dog, I make a great fuss of him when he brings his retrieve, and I hold the dummy as if I consider it a real prize. I have been told that Her Majesty the Queen says 'Thank you' to her dogs when they bring her a retrieve.

Occasionally canvas dummies become so grubby and slimy they need a wash, so I put them in plain water and give them a scrub with a stiff brush. When they dry out, they are a pleasure to use again and are fresh to your dog too.

Some people find it difficult to throw a dummy in a certain direction or for any distance. Practise without the dog around. Dummies with a string or rope on the end can make good throwing easier. A toggle often catches in your fingers so the dummy goes over your head; toggles also get caught easily on branches and vines. It is usually easier to be accurate if you throw underhand rather than overhand. Throwing from one side to the other across your body can also be very effective.

Retrieve articles. Some of the canvas dummies could do with a wash! The dummy launcher in the middle will throw a dummy many yards, the distance being governed by the strength of the .22 blank used.

THE SEEN RETRIEVE

Good marking is a great asset in a gundog. It saves time and energy – yours and the dog's. When your trained dog hears a shot, he should turn towards the sound, establish the direction of the shot, spot the quarry, mark its fall and keep his eyes on it. On his name alone, he should go as straight and as fast as his legs and the terrain permit, and collect the retrieve without further handling. It is pure joy to see a dog mark a long distance fall exactly and collect the retrieve at speed.

If you have an assistant to throw dummies for you, he or she should make a noise to attract the dog's attention just before he throws. A shrill 'Brrrrrr' noise seems to be traditional – I believe it is supposed to simulate a bird taking flight – or the thrower may say, 'Mark!' It should become a conditioned reflex in you that when you hear 'Brrrrrr' or 'Mark!' you say 'Sit' to your young dog. Your dog should learn to pay attention, and stop and look towards the sound immediately he hears it. The report of a starting pistol or dummy launcher should produce the same reactions in you both. In addition, you should teach him that the word 'Mark' means he should look in the direction you indicate with your hand.

In the very early stages you need to do all you can to make your dog steady to a thrown retrieve. He should wait for three things before he goes: for his name, the command, and a hand signal. He should not go on any one of these three things, but he must wait for each and all.

At this point you can kill two birds with one stone: build steadiness and teach the direction signal you will use later for unseen retrieves. Once the dog is truly steady, but not before, you may begin to send him on his name alone.

In the case of a young dog, we use the seen retrieve to teach him to respond to the direction signal, which will be used later on for unseens. Therefore you should give the signal with the little chop in it when first sending your dog for a seen retrieve. Later, when he has not seen the retrieve, he will be familiar with this hand signal as an indicator of the direction in which he must go when he has not seen the throw.

If you have already taught steadiness, you should not have to hold the dog by the collar or scruff. Whether you throw the dummy or you have an assistant, the following rule will apply: you watch the dog, and the dog will watch the dummy. You must prevent him from running-in, so watch him.

You will have established beforehand where you or your assistant mean the dummy to land, so it will be all right if you do not see where the dummy lands. In any case, if you are lucky, you will hear it land. Therefore when you are ready to send your dog, you will be able to give an accurate direction signal. Once the retrieve has been thrown, keep your eyes glued to your dog. Wait several seconds before sending him, and then be very calm and deliberate in your voice and actions. Place your hand alongside, almost touching, his muzzle. He will probably be looking intently towards the retrieve. If not, either nudge his face with your hand until he looks the right way, or place your thumb on top of his muzzle to stabilize it, and then move his head until it is pointing in the correct direction. Give a small chop of the hand along with your sending command and he should set off.

Many people use a sweeping forward motion of the hand to send their dog but I use this only for the delayed seen retrieve. The sweeping signal can be vague; the chop signal is only given when the dog is looking steadily in the direction you want him to go. Eventually you will want him to follow that direction, without deviating, until he finds scent or until you stop him for redirecting. This is called 'straight-lining' and, like good marking, saves a lot of time and energy.

Once you feel he is really steady, you can begin to send him for seen retrieves in a new way – that is, on his name alone. We adopt this new way because we do not want the dog to look away from the fall and lose his mark. No signal or command is given. It is most helpful to have someone else throwing for you.

Your thrower should make a noise such as 'Brrrrrr' or 'Mark!' just before he throws, and if the dog does not look his way, repeat the noise until he does look towards him. It sometimes helps to catch the dog's eye if the thrower slaps the dummy a few times. A second or two after the dummy lands, say your dog's name. At first, the dog will not go on his name alone because you have been making him wait for the three things before he is allowed to go. You will have to encourage him with a swish of the hand close to and past his face to start him moving. This is the signal you will use with the delayed seen, but will cease to use with the straightforward mark as soon as the dog will go on his name alone. Sometimes it helps if you take a step forward with the dog when you say his name. Say it enthusiastically.

What you do not want is the dog taking his eyes off the retrieve to look at you for instruction. Dogs will often do this even before the dummy has landed. You want him to keep his eyes fixed on the retrieve. If he looks up at you he will lose his mark; he may even miss seeing the actual fall. Put your left hand down beside his muzzle to keep his head still. If he resists this, hold his head with both your hands to keep him looking forwards. You may need to be very firm over this, as some dogs will strain to turn their eyes towards you even though their head is pointing forward. Your thrower will be a big help if he calls out until the dog looks and then throws straightaway. Once the dog sees the fall, say his name and encourage him with your hands to start him moving. After a few repetitions of this procedure, a dog will usually keep his eyes on the mark and be happy to set off to retrieve.

Another way to keep him looking forwards is for you to stand a pace ahead of him, though be sure not to obscure his view of the thrower. Once the dummy has landed, send him straightaway. You may lose some steadiness through sending him quickly, but you will be able to restore this as soon as the dog understands that he must keep his eyes on the fall.

Once the dog has got the idea of the marked retrieve, begin to increase the distance he has to mark. Most young dogs mark short. Marking short means that the dog begins to hunt for the retrieve before he reaches the right area. The trainer will be tempted to handle him or go out to help him, but this will delay the dog's development as a good marker. When your dog marks short, call him back to you. It may be difficult to get him to obey the recall as he is 'on a mission' and will not want to return. If necessary, you should go out towards him to make him realize you really mean it when you are calling him to you.

Ask your thrower to pick up the dummy, move your-

self and the dog closer, and ask for the dummy to be thrown again. Make sure the throw has enough height for the dog to see it from his level. It will also be helpful if the dummy falls on short grass in the early stages so that the dog sees it when he gets near. Continue to move towards the thrower each time the dog marks short. Once he succeeds, you can begin to extend the distance and arrange for the dummy to fall into longer grass. Your thrower may need to do a lot of picking up and re-throwing. You need someone who throws well and who is very patient – and you need to be very patient too. As he begins to succeed, your dog's confidence will grow and eventually he will go forwards until he finds scent or sees the dummy. The next step is to begin to lengthen the time between the dummy landing and you sending the dog. The dog must not look back at you. He must keep his eyes on the fall and wait to be sent. If he looks away from the fall, go back to the stage where you hold his head. If you are calm, patient and persevering, you will eventually succeed. Your dog will keep his gaze glued to the fall, and when cast, will go unerringly to the retrieve.

THE DELAYED SEEN RETRIEVE

I do not give a command for this, but some people use the word 'Fetch'. I use only the dog's name.

Delayed seen retrieves would consist of one or more seen retrieves, with a delay in sending for any of them. In my opinion, six or seven seconds would constitute a delay. If the dog looks away from the fall, I would treat this as a delay as well. In the case of a delayed single seen, the handler sends the dog on his name with a sweeping hand motion, or 'swish', to indicate the direction. In the case of two or more seens, the handler should sit the dog up facing the retrieve he wants, then send the dog on his name but with the swish to indicate the direction of the desired retrieve. The swish should be given with a flat hand starting alongside the cheek of the dog, and sweeping forwards past his face in the desired direction.

When a dummy is thrown or a bird is shot, your dog should keep his eyes fixed on the fall until he is commanded to go, or until his handler asks him to focus on him for another instruction. An example of the

ABOVE: The delayed seen. The dog is being sent with a 'swish' signal, and the handler has her eyes on the dog.

latter case would be when the dog has seen a dead bird fall, but the handler knows of a runner in another direction. Naturally, the runner must be collected before the dead bird. After the dog has brought you the runner, the dead bird is still there to be collected. This is a typical delayed seen retrieve. In this case, I use the dog's name together with the sweeping hand past and beyond his face, clearly indicating the direction – the swish signal. This tells him that it is the remembered but older seen bird he is to fetch.

The delayed seen retrieve method of casting the dog is used with what are called 'selected doubles', an exercise you will often encounter in working tests. Two dummies are thrown out and the judge will tell you the order in which the dog should retrieve them. Whichever dummy you are asked to send the dog for, you should make sure he is following your casting hand, so be sure you look at him as you send him. Indicate the direction, slowly and deliberately with your flat hand alongside his face, then send him with a swish of your hand past his face, together with his name.

You will also encounter this situation in a shooting context. The dog has seen two or more birds fall and

RIGHT: The delayed seen. Side view of the cast, with the handler watching the dog.

you want him to retrieve one as opposed to another, or you may wish him to retrieve each of them in a precise order for some reason. Be sure he is looking along your casting hand, and then send him on his name with the swish in the appropriate direction.

A technique that will help you in the situation where you wish the dog to pick a particular retrieve, as opposed to another, is to face him at heel looking towards each throw, or shot. Say 'Heel' as you turn him to face each throw, then say 'Sit, mark'. In a competition you will be told in advance the order in which the dummies are to be retrieved. If the first thrown of a double mark is to be retrieved first, you should sit the dog so he can clearly see the thrower of the second retrieve.

When the judge tells you that you may send your dog, turn him very deliberately, saying 'Heel', so that he faces the correct dummy. Insist that he sits square beside you looking in the right direction before you very carefully and deliberately cast him using his name and the swish. If your dog is at heel on your left and the forbidden throw is on the right, you can put yourself between him and his view of the dummy you do not want him to fetch. This will help in taking his mind off the unwanted dummy. If the forbidden dummy is on your left, it is more difficult, but by accentuating the turn away from that throw, and by being particularly vigilant and deliberate with your signal, you will achieve success.

Many handlers point to the unwanted retrieve and say 'No' or 'Leave' to their dog, but I prefer to say 'Heel', which is a positive command, and turn him away very decisively. The words 'No' and 'Leave' are too negative – you don't want him to think 'Never', you want him to remember the other retrieve for later.

When you first begin teaching selected doubles, make sure they are thrown at a wide angle to each other. They should be well spaced in distance from each other too, and you should be in a position to intercept the dog if he goes for the wrong one. The contrast between the two should be as marked as is practical. Make sure the dog brings the first dummy straight back to you. Many dogs will try to rush to the second dummy before delivering the first. Keep your concentration high and communicate with the dog. Give him lots of praise for doing it right. It is a tricky thing to scold the dog if

he goes wrong because you don't want him to think he is wrong to have the retrieve in his mouth! Dogs live in the moment.

As you receive the dummy from the dog, tell him to sit so that he registers the sit as the next action you require. You will then be in control and can set him up for the second retrieve.

With a young dog, if you send him for the last thrown dummy first, you are likely to be more successful than if you try for the first thrown. The second is fresher in his mind. However, this makes the second retrieve more of a memory test and sometimes a young dog will have forgotten the first throw entirely when you come to send him for it. If this is the case, you will need to treat the second retrieve as an unseen, and send him with the chop signal.

Even though you may decide that his first retrieve is to be the second throw, which makes it a straightforward seen retrieve, you should not send him on his name alone. He must be in no doubt as to which dummy you mean him to fetch. You must give him the swish signal along with his name. If he attempts to go for the wrong dummy, stop him and bring him back to heel. Take a step forwards with him, point him in the desired direction and try again.

If he succeeds in reaching the wrong dummy before you can stop him, just go out to him and take it from him. If possible, don't say a word until you have the dummy, then say 'Sit', and let him watch while you put it back in its place. If you do have to speak to him before you take the dummy and he complies with what you say, you will have to praise him, even though he has done wrong in picking the wrong dummy. If you do not have to speak to him, you can maintain a sterner demeanour. Once you have the dummy, say 'Sit' while you put it back in place, then say 'Heel' in a firm tone, and walk him back at heel to your starting point. Sit him facing towards the dummy you originally wanted, walk him several paces at heel in that direction, then set him up and send him on his name with the swish. When that retrieve is safely to hand, tell him to sit, and then, saying 'Heel', turn him and set him up to face the first thrown dummy.

If he persists on 'pulling' towards the unwanted dummy but you eventually get him to pick the correct one, do not let him have the second retrieve. Sit him and walk out and pick it up yourself. It is a good policy to pick up every fourth or fifth dummy yourself anyway so that he gets the idea that it is not always his turn.

If you succeed in getting him to fetch the correct dummy first without any bother, the second retrieve has now definitely become a delayed seen retrieve so you will send him with his name and the swish signal. If he seems to be acting dim about the second retrieve, give him the benefit of the doubt. He has probably forgotten about it. Leave him sitting and walk a few paces towards the dummy, then pretend to throw. Make your pretend throw convincing – you want your dog to get the message. Return to your dog and give him the swish signal along with his name. This should work, but if it does not, walk out with the dog, show him the dummy, perhaps moving it a little with your hand or foot to attract his attention, return to your start position, and send him once more, using the swish.

THE UNSEEN RETRIEVE

In a shooting situation it is sometimes impossible for the dog to see what has been shot. It may be a rabbit or a hare. Trees or other obstacles may be in the way. Rolling terrain may prevent either of you seeing what is shot. In these cases, it is a huge asset if the dog has 'gun sense'. This can only be acquired by a dog if he has seen a gun pointed and fired in the direction of the retrieve and has successfully found the retrieve several times. This type of retrieve should be treated as a 'blind' or unseen, and the chop sending signal should be used. A dog will also learn by experience that if he goes towards the sound of the shot and/or the sound of the fall, he has a good chance of finding. Often, he may find the place where shot has struck vegetation. This is usual in the case of ground game. With experience, he will learn to follow the direction of the bruising on the ground caused by the shot and this will lead him to the fall.

If there is any significant delay in sending for a seen retrieve, it should be classed as an unseen and treated accordingly. What is a significant delay? If in doubt, treat the retrieve as an unseen.

Training for the unseen retrieve requires a great deal of time and patience, but it is one of the most important and rewarding aspects of your dog's education. Initially things can be quite frustrating, but if you persevere with the methods described here you will succeed.

Command: I use 'Hie lost', which is a traditional, Old English command (or 'Fetch' or 'Find it').

Definition: 'Go in the direction indicated, and keep going until you find a retrieve or I redirect you.' In addition 'Hie lost' means 'Bring back the retrieve and hold on to it until I take it.'

How to do it: No matter how many seen retrieves you do with your young dog using the chop signal, he will not straightaway make the connection that he should go in the direction indicated when he has not seen a dummy thrown. At this stage you should certainly not use game. You will probably have to make many throws, and this will not be of benefit to a carcass or to the dog carrying it. Make sure you keep changing the dummies – do not keep throwing the same one.

There are two basic ways of teaching unseens. Whether you use one or both of these methods, this phase of your dog's training needs to be done in several small steps, just as with all the other aspects of his training.

The 'Blindfold' Method

Choose a day with a very light but steady breeze, and make sure to use the wind direction to the dog's advantage. Sit him at heel on your left and say 'Mark'. Throw the dummy forwards and when it is at the height of its trajectory, cover the dog's eyes. Do this by placing the thumb of your left hand over his near eye and your fingers over his far eye. The dog feels the swing of your body, sees the trajectory but only hears the fall. It is almost like a marked retrieve.

As soon as the dummy lands, let the dog see daylight. You do not want his pupils to dilate. Very deliberately, place your right hand alongside his muzzle, and saying 'Hie lost', give the little chop signal to cast him. He should be staring towards the fall, but if he looks towards you or upwards before you send him, guide

How to cover a dog's eyes – the right side. This is used when you don't want the dog to see where the retrieve lands.

How to cover a dog's eyes – the left side. The thumb covers the near eye, the fingers cover the far eye.

his muzzle with your hand until it is pointing the right way. Conversely, if he looks away from you, gently tap the side of his muzzle nearest you and he will turn towards you, then when he is looking straight, send him. When he finds the dummy, be very enthusiastic with your praise, then ensure that he comes straight back to you and makes a good delivery.

The next step is to cover his eyes before you throw. That is the only thing you change.

The following step is as the one before but as the dummy lands, you cough near the dog's ear. So he has heard 'Mark', has felt the swing of your body, but he has not heard the fall. He must rely mainly on your hand signal for direction.

When you have been successful with this, ask someone else to throw. When they are about to throw, they should say 'Brrrrrr!' or 'Mark', but that is the only clue the dog has, except that by now he realizes that if you cover his eyes, there is probably going to be a retrieve. The distance of your assistant's throw should not be more than your own throw to begin with, but gradually you can increase it. If at any point the dog does not seem to catch on and does not go straight off your hand when he is sent, go back a stage or two. For example, leave out the cough and let him hear the fall, or go right back to where you let him see the beginning of the throw, then cover his eyes. Remember, you can build on success but not on failure.

The 'Memory' Method

Another way to give your young dog the confidence to go out when he has not seen a dummy thrown is to use 'memory retrieves'. Take him at heel about thirty paces in a straight line. It is helpful if you have a hedge or fence on one side, and even more helpful if you have some kind of alley which will keep him straight. Let him see you throw a dummy forwards to land in short grass where it can be seen and where he will be able to catch the scent easily.

Walk back to your starting point with him, then turn and send him with 'Hie lost' and the chop signal. He should make the retrieve easily. If not, take him out again, pick up the dummy and let him see you drop it in the same place, walk him twenty paces back, then send him as before. This should do the trick, but if not, I would revert to the 'blindfold' method for a while.'

Gradually, using memory retrieves, you can extend the distance that he will confidently go. As you progress you should throw the dummy into more difficult places – rough grass or other light cover instead of on to bare ground. Next, begin to leave him halfway to the point where you go to throw the dummy, walk back, picking him up at heel on the way, and return to your starting place. Set him up and send him.

When he has done this well a few times, leave him sitting at the start point and let him watch you walk out twenty paces. Throw two dummies, one beyond the other about five paces apart. Go back and send him. He may pick the first or second dummy and he may swap, but do not worry about it. You may be able to prevent swapping if, as soon as you see him dip his head to pick one dummy, you blow the recall whistle to bring him back to you quickly. As with the selected double, make sure the dog brings you the first retrieve

The 'blindfold' method of teaching 'unseens'. The dog feels the swing of your throw and hears the fall. As soon as the dummy lands, let him see daylight so his pupils do not have time to dilate. He is sent for the retrieve with a clear chop signal and the command 'Hie lost'.

safely before he sets off for the next. When you have the first retrieve to hand, set him up very deliberately and send him for the second dummy.

Some dogs can be surprisingly slow on the uptake with this exercise so if your dog seems to have forgotten the second dummy, walk out with him encouraging him so that he finds it, then give him lots of praise. Alternatively, you could use the pretend throw. Remember to make it look convincing.

A variation on the memory theme is to let the dog watch you while you walk away from him about thirty or forty paces. Place a dummy on its end leaning on a tussock or against a bank, then walk around the area at the same distance from the dog, placing dummies at intervals of about thirty metres in an arc. Place the dummies virtually upright so that they will be visible to the dog. Return to him and line him up to face one of them. Place your hand alongside his face and say

'Mark'. Wait until he is staring at the dummy, then send him with 'Hie lost' and the little chop. Do this with each of the dummies in turn. When he has become consistently successful over, say, a few days, begin to extend the distance, change the order in which you send him, and gradually begin to place the dummies a little less upright. If he falters at any stage, go back to the previous level of success. Whichever method you are using, and of course you can use all, make sure to practise in several different places so that he understands that you always mean the same thing whenever you give that command and signal, whatever his surroundings. The picture the dog sees is so important to him.

DISTRACTIONS AND DIVERSIONS

We covered the subject of distractions and diversions fairly well in the section on steadiness. If the instinct to chase is engendered, your dog should stop, and if you blow your whistle or call, he should respond. There will be many occasions while your dog is retrieving when some distraction will present itself: a rabbit or hare may jump up from under his nose when he is on a retrieve, either on the way out or on the way back, or another bird may be shot, or another dog may run in while he is out working. Whatever the distraction, he should show that his control is beyond question.

You will have done a lot with tennis balls and dummies, but it is always difficult to simulate 'the real thing'. Find a heavy ball or a round stone about four inches in diameter. Paint a white spot about the size of a bantam egg on one side of the ball or stone. Walk with your dog at heel on lead with a downhill gradient on your left side. Without warning, toss the ball or stone across in front of your dog so that it rolls and bounces down the bank away from you. The white spot looks surprisingly like the scut of a rabbit and dogs seem to know instinctively what this is. Most dogs are really excited by this sight and will go to chase. Be ready for this and give a sharp tug on the lead, saying 'No! Sit'. Repeat the exercise until your dog understands that he must sit in response to the stimulus to chase, then do it without the lead. Do this exercise in different places so that he realizes that he must sit on each and every occasion.

Another very good temptation is a slice of log about four inches thick and six inches in diameter. The best sort has a few irregularities on the bark side so that it jumps and bounces when it is rolled along. Thrown across in front of your dog by an assistant, it is surprisingly effective – and cheap, too!

Make enquiries and hopefully you will find someone with a rabbit pen. The owner of the rabbit pen will be the one to help you make the best use of it. Alternatively, you should be able to find ground where rabbits abound to practise and teach your dog to react with self-control when he encounters bunnies.

You should also make friends with a gamekeeper and ask if you may accompany him when he is checking his pheasants while they are still in the release pen. At first you should stand outside the pen with your dog sitting at heel on the lead and let him watch the birds. Be strict over any undue interest, checking him and then saying 'Sit', as opposed to 'No' or 'Leave': you don't want him to think 'Never'. When you feel he has grasped what you want – that is, to watch but not to move – you will be able to leave him sitting, walk a short way, and then call him to you. After that you should progress to where you can call him in to heel while you are still walking away.

When you feel confident enough, ask if you may have him sitting with you inside the pen, watching the birds. Eventually you will be able to ask your dog to do a simple retrieve of a dummy in the pen. Make sure to throw it only a short distance and definitely not towards any birds – throwing it into a corner where you can be in a position to control your dog would be best. Only you will know when each change can be made; only you can know what your dog's reactions are likely to be. Err on the side of caution, and follow your instincts. It is important not to upset your keeper friend, nor to spoil your dog by going too fast.

Your dog must learn not to swap the retrieve he has in his mouth for another he sees on his way back to you. Equally, when he is on his way to a retrieve, he must remain on track in spite of any temptation to deviate for something else that comes into view on the way. This is not difficult to train for, but many handlers neglect this aspect of the dog's education.

Start by sitting your dog beside you at heel. Throw a

dummy out in front of you a good distance, say, thirty metres – if you have an assistant to throw for you, so much the better. Have another dummy under your left arm. Send your dog for the seen retrieve on his name alone. When he picks it and starts on his way back to you, let him see you gently throw out the dummy you still have at about 45 degrees behind you. He sees it clearly, but you are in a position to intercept him if he goes to pick it up. Speak to him, blow the recall, and do all you can to keep him coming to you, and make sure he gives you the retrieve. Try not to say 'No'. He may think you mean that he should not have the dummy in his mouth, and so drop it. He may well drop it anyway and attempt to go for the diversion. You may have to pick the diversion yourself, and if so, tuck it back under your arm and encourage him enthusiastically to bring you the correct dummy. Even when he brings the correct dummy, be sure to pick up the diversion yourself so the dog realizes it was not meant for him.

When he will return the correct dummy to you reliably, acknowledging but resisting the distraction, you can begin to throw the distraction out to one side of you. If successful in this, throw the distraction at 45 degrees to his path of return. When he really understands what you want, it will be possible for you to throw the distraction right into his path. The next phase is to place the distraction in his path a few yards from you just after he leaves you so that he comes across it unexpectedly on his return. Sometimes a dog will miss seeing it, but if he does spot it, he will be very surprised and interested. You will need to encourage him very enthusiastically to keep him coming with the original dummy. Moving away from the distraction as you call and encourage will be helpful.

A puppy following his handler over a 'jump' of a few logs.

OBSTACLES AND WATER

Command

The command for entering water or cover is 'Get in'; 'Over' is used to mean 'Negotiate that obstacle and get to the other side'.

Definition

When the retrieve is in water or cover, as opposed to the other side of a pond, river or obstacle, 'Get in' is used to convey this.

Your dog needs to learn to get over reasonable obstacles such as wooden fences and gates, through hedges, and over brooks and out of rivers on the far side. In these situations, 'Over' is used. While I do teach my dogs to jump wire fences, I think it is too tricky, not to say dangerous, to convey how it is done via the written word. Come and see me.

How To Do It

Negotiating Obstacles
While your Labrador is still a puppy – say, four or five

months old – it would not be too much to ask him to follow you over a narrow log, one of about six inches in diameter. Say 'Over' as he reaches it, and encourage him to follow you as you step over yourself. At this stage, you are just getting him used to acting in response to the word 'Over'.

As he matures physically, you can begin to encourage him to go over slightly higher but solid objects. Most dogs will jump on to the object and then over it, but it is preferable that he jumps without touching. Start to use a stick suspended over two blocks, which will appear to him as not substantial enough to take his weight. As you raise the height, drape a sheet or blanket over the stick to make it appear more of a barrier to the dog so as to deter him from running underneath. Most dogs love to jump and you can make a game of it; use edible rewards and you will find that your dog soon wants to show off how well he can jump. Do not use the retrieve in conjunction with jumping until your dog is a confident jumper, then use a tennis ball or something small which will not impede him in any way.

Negotiating Cover

Your Labrador needs to become confident in covert and in pushing through hedges. 'Get in' is your command here. You can start educating quite small puppies about pushing through cover by taking them through long grass and letting them find their own way. Dropping small biscuits into thicker stuff will encourage a youngster to push in – though be sure that the cover has no thorns, nettles or prickles. As time goes on, you can ask your young dog to retrieve a tennis ball from the same sort of cover, all in the spirit of play. If he is reluctant, send an older, more experienced but friendly dog, just to try and engender a little jealousy (the older dog must be friendly as you don't want him to round on your pup and bite or frighten him when he tries to join in).

Eventually you will want your dog to face more punishing cover. Some dogs are naturally more courageous than others, but if you find ways of making it worth his while, you should succeed. A greedy dog will respond to bribery, and a fanatical retriever will try hard for his prize. When it comes to 'the real thing', most dogs will enter dense cover if they can smell game scent.

Introducing Water

It is important for a gundog to enter water happily and to swim confidently, as there will be many occasions when the retrieve lies in or across a river or lake. Begin

The handler and an older dog giving youngsters confidence in water.

ABOVE: A careful entry into water.

BELOW: A confident leap into water.

ABOVE: A confident swimmer.

BELOW: The dummy is safely delivered and the dog shakes the water out of his coat.

to accustom your puppy to water at an early age. My puppies have a shallow paddling pool in their run which they enjoy playing in, especially when the weather is hot. It is easy to get into and out of so there is no fear of them drowning. Later, when they are able to go out and about, I take them with an older, confident, friendly dog to a shallow brook near my home. I wear my wellies and wade in with the older dog, encouraging the pups to follow and play in the water.

You should never force a young dog into the water – it will frighten him, and it may take a long time for him to get over it. Make certain there are no nettles on the bank as they sting much more strongly when the dog is wet and he may well associate the stinging with the water. Be sure that it is easy for the pup to climb out of the stream or he may panic and be afraid to go in again. Encourage the youngster to go out of the water on the far side by throwing a biscuit ahead of him and saying 'Over'. A tennis ball is also a good lure. However, you should stand in the water to take it from him so that the ball comes straight from his mouth to your hand. This is a good habit to instil, and leads to a good delivery from water later on. Don't give him the opportunity to shake and perhaps drop the ball: it is preferable that the dog shakes after the retrieve is safely in your hand.

DIRECTING THE DOG AT A DISTANCE

Directing the Dog to the Side

Commands
For right and left, the words 'Right' and 'Left' are being used more and more commonly. Of course, this would mean 'Stage right' and 'Stage left' for the dog: it is important not to say 'Go left' or 'Go right', because when the dog hears the word 'Go' he may well choose to go in the direction he pleases. Just keep to 'Left' or 'Right'.

Some handlers use 'Get out' for one side and 'Get on' for the other. Again, I think it is a mistake to incorporate the word 'Get' in either command as the dog will hear 'Get' and go which way he chooses – dogs are so quick! So if you prefer this to 'Right' and 'Left', just say 'Out' or 'On'. However, you should consider whether you also use the word 'Out' to tell the dog to go or stay

out of a room or enclosure. Whereas you can use one word to mean a combination of things, you must not use any word to mean two utterly different things. If you think that using 'Right' and 'Left' is too much like a circus trick and makes you feel self-conscious, you could say 'Away' and 'Bye'. Saying 'Right' or 'Left', or other words for the direction you want, has the distinct advantage that if your dog cannot see you, or has the sun in his eyes, he can respond to your voice command and change direction. Some of my dogs understand the direction commands so well, I can stand with my hands in my pockets – nice on a very cold day – and blow the 'stop' whistle, then when the dog stops, I just use my voice. Some people are already using a whistle signal to make their Labrador change direction, just as spaniel and sheepdog trainers do. However, it seems that many Labradors have to be stopped before they can react to a change of direction command or signal – they seem to be incapable of changing direction while on the move.

Hand Signals
As has been said already, each signal must be absolutely clear so that the dog has no scope for interpreting it to his own designs. Your arm in your sideways signals should come up from your side and go straight out to its full extent. If you already have your hand raised in the 'sit' signal, you should use the same hand to indicate the required direction. In other words, you will know before you stop him which way you wish the dog to go, so if it is to the left, your left hand should be used to give the 'sit' signal, and vice versa.

I tend not to use the 'sit' hand signal unless I really wish to settle the dog before directing it. I prefer to raise the appropriate arm, straightened, to shoulder height before I blow the 'stop' whistle, and then when the dog stops and turns to look at me, I waggle my outstretched hand and say 'Right' or 'Left'. This makes the dog more willing to stop and look because he receives information as soon as he does so.

You will sometimes see a handler give his dog a very contradictory signal. Let's say he wants to send his dog to the right. He has successfully stopped his dog and it is looking at him. He raises his right hand in front of him and brings it across his body towards the left and then throws it out to the right, moving his whole body sideways in emphasis. The dog goes left. Dogs are so quick, and this dog has seen the slight movement of the hand to the left, and off he goes in the belief that he is correct. But the signal was ambiguous, and the handler has only himself to blame. Be clear.

Definition

Whichever commands you use, you will accompany them, especially in the beginning, with a hand signal. The word will then mean, 'Go in the direction indicated, until you find something or you receive another command.'

How To Do It

We touched upon this in the section on the 'sit', as 'Sit' and direction signals go hand in hand.

You should use every opportunity to blow the 'stop'

whistle – when you are going to feed your dog his dinner or just give him a treat, when you are going to throw a dummy, when you are going to give him a hand signal. Any time you want him to sit and look at you, use the 'stop' whistle and make it worth his while by giving him, or showing him, something.

Before he is reliable on the 'stop' whistle at any great distance, you can begin direction training by sitting him on the whistle facing you, then throw a dummy out to his side. Tell him to sit, and carefully move away from him at right angles to the dummy. Only go a few paces, then blow your 'stop' whistle with your hand up in the 'sit' signal. Use the hand that you will use for the direction signal and say 'Sit' firmly.

This next bit is very important. Your dog will guess that you are about to send him for the dummy he has seen, and may start moving as soon as you touch your whistle. You must prevent this, so keep saying 'Sit' in a firm but friendly tone while you carefully stretch out your arm to the side. When your arm is almost fully extended, say 'Left' or 'Right' as appropriate, and waggle your hand. That is his moment to go.

The point of doing things in this way is to ensure that the dog sees the whole signal. If he anticipates and goes before he sees your arm fully extended and your hand waggling, later, when you are doing unseens and stop him and give the hand signal, he will not know what it means because he has never seen it.

It is very common that when you first do this exercise, the dog looks puzzled and comes towards you. This is because he is used to being sent from beside you and he thinks it cannot be right to set out to retrieve from another position. The same thing usually happens when the dog is away from you and you start trying to teach him to go further away. This is discussed in the next section. However, quite soon he realizes that it is permitted to set off in a direct line to the retrieve: 'The shortest distance between two points is a straight line.'

Directing the dog to the side. A clear, unambiguous, shoulder-height left arm signal. Always ensure that your dog sees the whole of each signal, especially in the early days.

Directing the dog to the side. A clear, unambiguous, shoulder-height right arm signal. The handler must take care to point a parallel line to the line which the dog must travel to reach the retrieve.

Please note that your sideways arm signal should not point at the retrieve. You should be indicating a parallel line to the line the dog must travel to reach the retrieve. Imagine this: suppose that the dog is at 100 metres from you, and the dummy or bird is about two metres downwind of him. If you point at the retrieve, it will appear to the dog that you are almost pointing at him, and this will confuse him. Your signal must be absolutely clear. If you point a parallel line to the line the dog needs to travel it will be clear: the dog will move in the right direction and soon come into a position where he can find the retrieve.

Meanwhile, you should be teaching the dog that he must stop on the 'stop' whistle instantly whenever he hears it. You know that he can react instantly, so insist that he does. If he is slow, do not remain rooted to the spot, but go out to him, put the lead on and take him back to the point where he was when he heard the whistle. To do this you must remember the exact spot yourself. Identify it by some clump of grass or a flower as you blow the whistle. The dog will know if you get it wrong, and if you give him an inch, he will take a mile. Once you have him on this spot, be kind, blow the whistle – not in his ear – the same length as usual, and praise him. Remember, you want a willing worker – you want him to *want* to do what you want him to do.

The next step is to give the dog the release command and allow him to run about near you. When he is about three metres from you, blow the 'stop' whistle, and when he is seated, throw a dummy out to his side. Remind him to sit, and blow the whistle again while you carefully move further away. When you are about seven or eight paces from him, face him and blow again. When he looks at you, give the arm signal, making sure that he waits to see the whole signal, and give your command to go just at the end of the signal.

Most of us are strongly left- or right-handed, so you must be sure not to neglect the less strong side. Ring the changes and teach both left and right equally well.

Soon you should be able to throw out two dummies, one to each side, each prefaced by the 'stop' whistle. Move away from him, blow again, and send the dog for the dummy you choose. Make sure he remains still until he has seen the whole signal. If he goes for the wrong dummy, go back a phase so that there is only one to fetch, then when you return to having two out, send him for the one he seems keenest to go for, probably the last thrown. Each time you have success, be really enthusiastic with your praise – it will accelerate progress.

When you feel he has a real grasp of the meaning of the signals, begin using the 'blindfold' method again to make the transition from seen to unseen. Sit the dog using the whistle, cover his eyes, say 'Mark', throw the article and let him hear it fall. Let him see daylight. Blow the 'stop' whistle again. Walk away at right angles for, say, ten paces, turn, and blow the 'stop' whistle again. When the dog is looking at you, give the arm signal and command, making sure he sees the whole signal, and off he should go in the right direction. Repeat the performance in the opposite direction.

After this you can begin to throw when his eyes are covered but cough so he cannot hear the fall. Following this, you continue along similar lines to those used when you were teaching the dog to go out on unseen dummies. Ask someone else to throw for you so the dog only hears 'Mark', and the fall and so on.

Teaching direction signals when the dog is in water is slightly trickier than when he is on land. You have to be very quick. You are going to teach him that the 'stop' whistle means the same in water as it does on land. The same goes for your hand signals.

Your dog should be fairly confident in water. Sit him on the bank. Throw a stone out a good way, say, twenty metres or more. The stone is to get him started, but then you are going to want him to obey the 'stop' whistle. If he should ignore you and keep going, he will not get the reward of a retrieve. Send him into the water and when he has gone only a very short distance, blow the 'stop' whistle and reinforce it with your command, 'Sit!' and perhaps 'Mark!' and 'Brrrrr!'. Do all you can to get his attention.

You will probably have to work really hard to get him to stop and turn to look at you, but immediately he does, throw a dummy out about ten metres to the side. He will of course set off straightaway to fetch it. You must instantly blow the 'stop' whistle to make him look at you. Again, you will need to use your voice and be very emphatic and active in order to gain his attention. You may have to run along the bank parallel to him; keep trying to get him to look at you. You want him to fetch, but you want him to see the signal that goes with the direction. Have your signal arm outstretched and ready so that if he so much as glances at you he will see the signal and then continue towards the dummy.

This exercise seldom goes smoothly, but after practising for a while, you will find he becomes more willing to look your way in response to the whistle, and soon you should feel you could throw out two dummies in opposite directions, prefacing each one with the 'stop' whistle. The whistle has come to mean, 'Look at me, I'm going to show you something you want to see.' As he sees the second throw, blow again. As he looks at you, have your hand signal ready to send him to retrieve.

Many of the skills your Labrador has to learn will blend in with more than one aspect of his training. Most dogs adapt easily to a new situation, realizing that the same command or signal fits into a different context. However, much of your training will consist of taking the dog around to different places and doing the same exercises in order to make him understand that commands and signals mean the same even though the surroundings are different. The picture means so much to the dog.

Directing the Dog to Go Further Away

Command

The command for this exercise is 'Get on', pronounced 'Giddawn' ('On', 'Out' or 'Away'), and is used to tell the dog he needs to go further away from you. Usually this direction is harder to teach than the sideways ones, which is a puzzle to me. When you have taught a dog the release command his one idea seems to be to go as far away as possible!

Many people use the word 'Back', but to me this sounds too much like 'bad!'. I do use the word 'Back' to mean 'Get behind me' when, for instance, we are walking on a very narrow path or footbridge. I also use it in a non-working situation, for instance to tell a dog to get from the front of the car into the back – get behind me – if he has jumped over the seats – which in a way does signify 'bad'! Another reason I do not like the use of 'Back' is that when you have a whistle in your mouth, which you should do from the moment before you cast the dog from your side, you cannot say 'Back' properly

– you are like a poor ventriloquist who says something in the order of 'Gack'!

The commands 'Get on', 'Away' or 'Back' are not for use when casting the dog from beside you, but only when he is at a distance and has to go further from you. The reason for this is that if you use the same command for two different things, it is confusing to the dog and it will take you longer to make him understand. It can be done, but why confuse him? Similarly, some handlers use 'Back' for left and right as well as straight on, but this leads to the dog choosing to go in the direction he pleases.

Hand Signals

Your hand should be raised vertically from in front of your chest, until it is as high as you can reach, ending with a distinct upward flick. This is a movement of about a metre, and is easily discerned by a dog even at a great distance. I remember being on a grouse moor in Scotland some years ago, and a pricked bird had glided on some 300 metres and lay, a tiny speck in the distance, the far side of a valley. My dog, Shadow, had not seen it go, but I was able to handle her out, and it was obvious that she could see the signal even at the furthest point. What a thrill it was to see her returning, the white feathers showing that she had been successful. The Guns put her retrieve in the game book.

There are two other direction signals used when requiring the dog to go further away. The command is the same as for directing the dog to go straight away from you, but the hand signal is slightly different. If, for example, you need the dog to go away at an angle of around 45 degrees to the left, raise your left hand and give your flick at 11 o'clock. To send him away at approximately 45 degrees to the right, raise your right hand and give the flick at 1 o'clock.

Definition

The command 'Get on', or 'Giddawn' – which is my command of choice – is used for telling the dog to go further away when he is not far enough out. Initially the command means 'Go straight away', but later in training your modified hand signal, coupled with the command, will mean go further away at 11 o'clock or 1 o'clock.

How To Do It

By introducing the retrieve early on in the teaching of the 'sit' whistle, you will get the idea across to the dog that it is worthwhile stopping and looking at you. Once he will stop and look at you, you can make good progress with the direction signals.

There are several ways to do this. In the very beginning, I send the dog out on the release command, and when he is only a few yards from me, I blow the 'stop' whistle and give the 'sit' hand signal. When he is sitting, I produce a dummy from my bag and waggle it a bit. I blow the 'stop' again. The dog should be looking at me because for some days now I have been showing him things as a sort of reward for sitting. I keep my hand up in the 'sit' signal – remember, no higher than your forehead – and saying 'Sit', I slowly throw the dummy out beyond him.

I say 'slowly' because I don't want the throw to be too exciting, and you must be sure not to hit the dog with the dummy. You can throw the dummy a little to one side, then move yourself so that the dog is in a direct line from you to the dummy. I blow the stop whistle again. When the dog looks at me, I throw my arm up in the signal I use for sending the dog straightaway and say 'Get on'. Some dogs that have not heard the command or seen this signal before seem confused and remain sitting, but if you add 'Hie lost!' and encourage him, he should soon catch on to what is wanted.

Your dog needs to see the whole of your signal. Because he has seen the dummy and knows where it is, he may well be off like a whippet as soon as he sees the smallest part of your signal, but you must make him remain sitting until you have shown him the whole signal. To do this, you must move very slowly, repeating 'Sit' over and over as you raise your arm. When your arm is fully extended, give the final flick as you say your command to go.

If the dog sees only the first part of the signal, he will not know what the real signal looks like in its entirety. Thus later on, when he stops to take direction and turns to look at you, obviously you will show him the whole signal – but if he has never seen it all, he will not recognize it, and he will not know how to respond.

Stopping a dog on the way out to a retrieve, and

then signalling and commanding him to go on, can create problems. You may not succeed in stopping the dog, thereby letting him think he can disobey, or you stand the risk of making him sticky on the outrun. It is better to use the 'blindfold' and the 'memory' methods to progress from seen to unseen. Remember to extend the distances gradually, and always insist on a good delivery.

Keeping the Dog in an Area

Command

The command in this case is 'Steady' or 'There'. Many people use a whistle signal for this too. I use a soft two-toot sound that sounds a bit like saying 'Steady', but is drawn out, as in 'Ste-dee'.

Definition

The definition for this manoeuvre is 'You are coming into a position, or you are in a position, where you should be able to wind (smell) the retrieve.' If you know where the retrieve lies and can keep your dog in a tight area near it, you will be giving him the best chance of finding it, even in difficult scenting conditions. Scent is affected by many things; wind, heat, frost, humidity, rain, other people or animals present or recently nearby can all cause disturbance or masking of scent.

How To Do It

Choose a grassy field with tufts or features such as dock leaves. Sit your dog, then walk away and gently toss a tennis ball into one of the tufts, or a spot you can identify even if you take your eye off it. Go back to the dog and send him out to retrieve using the swish (delayed seen signal). As he approaches the area, say your command. He will almost certainly go straight to the spot but even so say 'Steady' as he approaches it.

In the future, you should always try to be sure that the dog is coming into a downwind position in relation to the retrieve before you give the command – that is, a position where scent is blowing from the article towards him. Your dog needs to be able to trust you when you tell him that he is coming into a position where he will be able to find the article. You must try to tell him the truth.

The next stage is to cover the dog's eyes as you throw the ball. Try to make it land in much the same place as before. Send the dog and say 'Steady', as before. If he finds the ball on

Sending the dog further out. The command is 'Get on', and the hand signal is raised from in front of your chest to as high as you can reach, ending with an upward flick.

your command, well and good; if, however, he goes wide or too far beyond it, say 'No' softly, and encourage him to return to the correct area. As he comes into a position where he should find it, say 'Steady' again. It's a bit like that game we used to play as children where the person who hid the article watches the seeker and says, 'You're getting warmer, warmer, boiling hot, no, colder now, colder, freezing!' You may need to go towards the tennis ball in order to encourage the dog to return to the area, but give him all the help you can so that he succeeds. It's a very good thing for the dog to think that you know more than he does and can help him. Knowing more than he does in this game is a state that doesn't last long, and quite soon he knows a lot more than you do because of his superior scenting abilities!

THE DELIVERY

Command

The command for the delivery is 'Dead' (or 'Drop'). Do not use 'Give' because that sounds too much like 'Leave', which means 'Have nothing to do with that!'

Definition

The definition for the delivery is 'Put it in my hand', and the most important thing about the delivery is to get the retrieve in your hand. Your Labrador's prime function is to retrieve runners so that they can be quickly and humanely dispatched. In most cases this means birds – partridge, pigeon, pheasant, duck, grouse – but it also means hares and rabbits. If, when the dog reaches you, he releases the wounded quarry, it is possible that neither you nor the dog will catch it again. By the time a bird or other animal has been shot and spent a minute or more in a dog's mouth, it will be teeming with adrenalin, and if it gets away from the dog, it will shoot off and may well escape for good, especially if it is a duck near water. It really is important, therefore, that your dog delivers to hand. The dog must realize that the retrieve, in all cases, is your property: it is a privilege that he is allowed to collect, look after and bring it to you.

How To Do It

The perfect delivery is when your dog carries his retrieve well balanced in his mouth straight back from the fall to you, holds his head up and places the prize in your hand. Unhappily there are several alternatives. He may deviate after picking it up and go off on a private mission with the retrieve in his mouth. He may bring it nearly back to you, then drop it on the ground. He may bring it right up to you but refuse to give it to you, or he may circle you and invite you to chase him for it.

The dog that runs off with the retrieve is showing his lack of focus on you, and you need to reinstate yourself as his centre of attention. Stop practising the retrieve and take him back to doing the recall really well. Insist on an immediate response to your voice and to the whistle, whether he is on the move or coming from the sit. A dog that will come will bring. Each time he returns to you give him enthusiastic praise and occasionally a titbit.

When you feel he is truly reliable on the recall – and you must be honest with yourself about this – begin again with simple retrieves in a confined area. This should be no bigger than a tennis court, but should have some sort of rough grass or low cover. Throw or place the dummy and send him for it. As soon as you see your young dog lower his head to pick up the dummy, blow the recall and call him enthusiastically to return to you. Your command is *'Come'*, not 'Bring it', 'Hold' or anything else. When he arrives, praise him enthusiastically, letting him hold the dummy for several seconds if he will before you take it.

If he deviates on his way back to you, he needs to be told immediately that you do not like it. However, you have to be careful not to sound too cross as you do not want him to think that he is wrong to have something in his mouth. The situation may be very ticklish.

It is very naughty, indeed maddening, of a dog to stop and cock his leg when he is on his way back with a retrieve. Perhaps it is your fault for not giving him a chance to have a wee beforehand, or perhaps his hormones are in control. I think you can scold him for this, because cocking his leg is uppermost in his mind, and the retrieve in his mouth is secondary. If

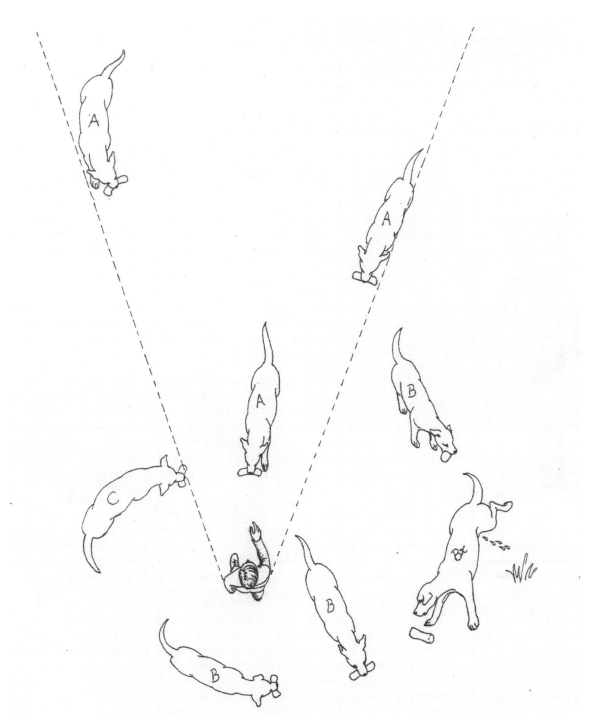

The delivery. Good dogs and naughty dogs: The 'A' dogs returning to the handler from in front within a narrow angle of, say, 45 degrees, are good and should receive enthusiastic praise. The 'B' dogs are naughty and should be spoken to in a warning voice. 'Bx' is especially naughty and should be scolded in a cross voice. 'C' is coming right and his handler should start to praise him with enthusiasm.

The delivery. The wrong way to appear to a dog returning with a retrieve. Seeing the palms of the handler's hands causes a dog to drop the retrieve on the ground more than any other thing.

looks like the open mouth of a puppy begging for food, which causes the mother or other adult members of the pack to regurgitate food to the pup, but I do not think that this is the reason your dog spits out the dummy. It may be that showing the palm looks too eager and perhaps a bit threatening to the dog, so he spits out the retrieve so as not to be involved with the 'handover'.

Whatever the reason, the remedy is simple: do not show the dog your palms. When your dog comes back with a retrieve, stand relaxed with your hands hanging loosely beside you. When he reaches you, extend your hand to pat him on the head, just as you would when

he ever cocks his leg during training, I would admonish him – there is a time and a place for everything! You will have to weigh up what is uppermost in your dog's mind before you scold him. Using the muzzle-holding technique before and during training is likely to be beneficial with this sort of dog as it should make him more respectful of you.

There is no one thing that makes a dog more likely to drop the retrieve before he reaches his handler than seeing the palms of the hands, and I am not sure why this is. It could be that the dog perceives them as confrontational, or it may be because the palm is what he sees when he is about to receive a smack, but even dogs that are not smacked will drop the dummy when they see the handler's palms. It may be that the palm

The delivery. Correct – the handler stands and waits for the dog, upright and relaxed.

The delivery. Correct – the handler extends the hand, the palm facing down.

Another thing which makes a young dog spit out the dummy is if he is scolded for having something in his mouth that you do not want him to have. This might be carrion or some valuable item of clothing. What you should do is call the dog to you and take the article as you would any other retrieve article. To him a retrieve is a retrieve. Once a young dog has something in his mouth, you need to be really careful about what you are teaching him, and what pathways are being formed in his mind.

Of course, if you have had to take a cowpat or a very dead rabbit from your dog, you will have a truly repellent smell on your hands. You may try soap, detergent, hand cream – nothing seems to get rid of

he answers the recall and comes without anything in his mouth. You would do this with your palm facing down towards the ground. If this is what he sees on his return to you, he will almost certainly continue to hold the dummy or, later, the game. You then slide your hand down towards his mouth, and saying 'Dead', take the retrieve overhand. It's almost sleight of hand, like a magician.

The next most common thing that will cause a dog to drop the dummy is the handler telling him to sit before he takes delivery. Sitting for delivery is required in obedience tests, but not for gundog work. The most important thing in a shooting context is to get the retrieve in your hand.

The delivery. Correct – the handler reaches past the dog's ear as if to pat her on the head.

The delivery. Correct – the handler curls her hand over and round the end of the dummy.

it. Don't despair, because there is something: cold, used teabags. Squeeze these in your hands for a few minutes, then wash your hands with soap again – the teabag treatment will make a marked improvement.

Telling your dog off for running-in can make him drop the dummy instead of giving it to you. His instinct to retrieve can be so strong that he is compelled to go and fetch in spite of your rating him, but when he returns, if you cannot suppress your displeasure, he will either drop it short of you, or circle you with it and refuse to come up close to you.

If you have not prevented him from running-in, you must cease scolding him the instant he dips his

head to pick up the retrieve. You must change your whole demeanour from anger to, if not pleasure, at least nonchalance. He must not be reprimanded for having things in his mouth. Go out to meet him, take the dummy without a word, then say 'Sit', and replace the dummy where it should be. Walk him back at heel to your starting place, and after an interval send him on command and try to achieve a good delivery when he returns.

If the dog persists in dropping the dummy on the ground in spite of all your care to avoid the things mentioned above, you must change the picture he sees

The delivery. Correct – saying 'Dead', the handler takes the dummy overhand. The sit is optional.

when he returns to you. Try turning your face away, and keep your hands in your pockets or behind your back until he is right up close to you. Or you can crouch or even lie down. When he reaches you, share the dummy with him, take it and give it back to him, take it again, make him know that you are delighted with him. Let your hair down.

Something else that works is to walk away when you see the dog has the retrieve and is on his way back. He will be keen to catch up with you. When you perceive the dog is nearing you, keep walking but reach down and gently pat him on the head. Be sure to keep walking. If the dog overtakes you, turn away from him and keep walking. Also turn away from anyone else who is with you – you do not want the dog to worry that someone else or their dog is going to steal the retrieve. Eventually, if you have been successful in patting him, you should be able to slide your hand from the top of his head to the end of the dummy and hold it. Encourage the dog to keep hold of it too, so that you are sharing it. Keep up your praise all the while. You are praising the dog for keeping the retrieve in his mouth. If he drops it on the ground, withdraw your favour and start walking again. He may leave it but you should just send him back for it and keep walking.

It is our instinct to pick up anything we see fall to the ground. I suppose this stems from a time when food was scarce and we became quick to pick up anything that dropped. We must train ourselves out of this. You should never accept a retrieve from the ground. If you feel you are fighting a losing battle, or are running out of time or patience, cover the dog's eyes and pick up the dummy yourself and put it out of sight before you uncover his eyes. He must not see you pick up the dummy.

At any point, if your dog drops his retrieve, even if he drops it because you have fumbled taking it, you must not let him see you pick it up! If you do, he will think that that is what is supposed

The delivery. Incorrect – the handler looks over-eager, and the dog ducks her head to avoid the hands.

The delivery. Incorrect – the handler's stance is overwhelming and the dog's demeanour becomes reluctant.

to happen. The picture matters so much to him. He will think it is your job to pick it up, when in fact it is his job to hold on to the retrieve until you are ready to take it. You may be shooting, for instance: you send him for a runner, and then dozens of birds begin to come over. He must look after the bird he has retrieved until you have finished shooting and are ready to take delivery.

Our instinct is to get the 'prize' as quickly as possible, and often this leads to us snatching the dummy,

and most dogs do not like this. Act nonchalantly. There was a very well known Dorset gentleman called Pop Bailey who was an extremely talented dog trainer. He has gone to the Happy Hunting Ground now, but I can see him in my mind's eye standing next to me chatting while his little Springer was off collecting a dummy. Pop had a prosperous build and he had his hands folded on top of his tummy. Presently the little dog returned with his prize. Pop gave no sign that he had noticed; he just kept chatting away. The spaniel started to bounce up and down at his owner's feet, trying to attract his attention. Eventually Pop looked down over his tummy, hands still folded comfortably there, and said, 'Hello, little dog. What 'e got there then?' By now the dog was frantic to give the dummy to Pop. He stood up on his hind legs and lifted the dummy as high as he could. Pop uncurled one hand and took the retrieve and said, 'Good boy!' All Pop's dogs had a good delivery, and I am sure this was mainly due to his being utterly relaxed about the whole thing and pleased to receive the retrieve.

If you appear to the dog to be too eager to have the prize, he can be overwhelmed and you will not have a good delivery.

The more difficult a retrieve is to find, the more respect a dog seems to show it and the better his delivery. Sending a dog repeatedly for dummies on terrain which is like a croquet pitch is too easy, and will lead to him playing with the retrieve, throwing it down or refusing to bring it to you. Choose rough grass with tussocks, and make retrieves progressively more difficult and tricky.

Retrieves from water need special treatment in order to achieve a good delivery. As your dog swims back with the retrieve, watch to see where he is planning to come ashore and go there to meet him. Keep your face slightly averted so as not to be confrontational in any way. You will still be able to see him. If you can step into the water safely so that you can take the retrieve while the dog is still in the water himself, say, up to his underbelly, you should do so. If you can take delivery before the dog pauses to shake the water out of his coat, you will be building a good habit. It is most unfortunate if the dog drops the dummy or bird in order to shake, as this soon becomes a bad habit. In the case of a wounded duck, neither you nor the dog are likely ever to recover it without someone having to shoot the creature on the water first.

Be lavish with your praise when the dog gets it right. Once the dog realizes how pleased you are when he puts the retrieve in your hand, he will want to do it the way that earns him the praise. Later, when he understands how pleased you are when he puts the retrieve in your hand, you can begin to take it in a more relaxed way. It is natural for us to extend our hand palm upwards to receive an article, but we can just as easily learn to put our hand out as we do when shaking hands with another person, that is, with the palm facing sideways.

There are trainers who advocate a type of force training whereby they place the dummy in the dog's mouth and hold the mouth shut while they repeat the word 'Hold'. I do not like this method, or the use of 'Hold' – and if a judge hears this word, he knows immediately that you have had a problem. The dog that needs to be trained by force will not be reliable when out of sight. If your dog refuses to pick up dummies or balls, try him on a toy or bone. Try anything you can think of to get him to retrieve naturally. When he understands that you are pleased with him for carrying things – and you should act as though you are absolutely thrilled – he will *want* to do it, and he will be happier to carry other objects. If you feel the need to use a word or phrase meaning 'Keep it in your mouth', use 'Hie lost': this makes sense because the command means, 'Go and find the retrieve, bring it back and hang on to it until I say "Dead".'

Some dogs hang on to the retrieve and will not give it to the handler. They will sometimes clamp their jaws so tightly you may worry that they are hard-mouthed, and indeed it could lead to this. Common causes include using the same dummy over and over, making the retrieves too easy, and a lack of respect for you. This last can often be remedied merely by using the muzzle-holding technique before you start a training session, repeating it often during the session, and especially just before you send him for the retrieve. What you are telling the dog is that you are in charge and that he should acknowledge your leadership. Furthermore, it is not his article, it is yours.

Put a flat, buckle-on collar on his neck. If you have taught him to come reliably, he will bring the retrieve right up to you. This being so, you can then take hold of the collar which means you have both dog and retrieve. Say 'Dead', take hold of the end of the dummy, and place your other hand over his eyes. This often works with a submissive type of dog as it makes him feel disadvantaged, not so possessive, so he is happier to give up the dummy. If it does not do the trick, take hold of the end of the dummy with one hand and put the thumb or a finger of your other hand in his mouth behind the dummy and press down on his tongue. This usually causes a slight gag reflex and you can slip the dummy out of his mouth quickly, making sure to praise him, and repeating the word 'Dead'.

If this fails, a tougher approach is needed. Give the command, take hold of the end of the dummy, and place the other hand over his muzzle. Press his upper lip hard against his teeth. This discomfort should make him draw back and release his grip so that you can quickly remove the dummy. Make a huge fuss of him, interspersing your praise with the word 'Dead'. Next, put the lead on and put him in his quiet place.

Occasionally a dog will not give up the retrieve except by bribery. I hate to resort to this, but it is better to exchange a biscuit for the prize than to risk the dog becoming hard-mouthed through your using harsher and harsher methods. It is so important to get over any problem without delay. Act quickly, decisively and physically, because the longer a problem persists, the firmer the pathway in the brain becomes, and the more difficult it is to eradicate.

Each time you receive the retrieve, keep it in your hand in a relaxed way. The dog must not try to snatch it, and you must not whisk it away behind your back. After all, it is yours. He has been allowed to fetch it, but it is your property and he has no right to take it from you. If he keeps trying to take it from you, say 'Dead', and put your free hand over his muzzle to remind him who is boss. Try not to say 'No', because you do not want him to think 'Never'. The dummy should be held as it will be when the dog has abandoned interest in grabbing it. He may succeed in taking hold of it, but use the above ways to make him release it, and praise him when he does. You should not permit a tug-of-war to develop. Having a collar on his neck will enable you to prevent this.

CHAPTER 10

PUTTING IT ALL INTO PRACTICE

As you will now know, most of dog training is joining up very small parts to make the whole. I consider that every small change, every step we take, is part of a pattern, a sort of web or chain mail made of very fine, strong links, all dependent on each other. These links represent the very small increments in the progress of training, the very gradual nature by which the dog gains understanding of what we want. The web is the spread of knowledge gained by the dog which makes him into a well rounded gundog. Parts of the training regime may seem tedious at times, but if each link is put carefully and firmly in place, the result is worth the time and effort.

When you feel that your dog is focused on you and that he is under control, you will want to move things forward. Both you and your dog will benefit from a little challenge, and one idea is to enrol for training classes.

TRAINING CLASSES

Most gundog clubs hold training classes during the summer. The Kennel Club can provide you with a list of clubs that hold field trials in Britain; you can then contact the secretary of your nearest society and ask about classes. If there are no classes within reasonable reach of you, ask if there is a local trainer they could recommend who might help you. There are good

Training class. Dogs and handlers practising heelwork. (Courtesy Paul Quagliana, Shooting Times)

Training class. The handlers have left their dogs in the 'sit'. The instructor's dog has moved and is being replaced on his spot. (Courtesy Paul Quagliana, Shooting Times*)*

trainers and poor trainers, and you will have to find out for yourself if you can get on with a person, and if what they tell you is going to be helpful to you.

Training classes have several benefits. They will give you a new place in which to practise. The instructor will organize you, and probably throw or hide dummies for you. You will be able to arrange it so that your dog hears bangs – probably a starting pistol or dummy launcher – at a distance to begin with, then closer. Your dog will see keen dogs become excited by bangs, and will watch them retrieve as a result of a bang. The element of competition, even jealousy, will give him a stronger interest in his training. Your instructor will give you ideas to help overcome any hiccups you may have with training. You will probably be given some homework to do between classes.

One of the best aspects of classes is the social side, both for you and your dog. You will meet like-minded people, and your dog will learn to behave in company. You will swap ideas – we are a great species for trading information! A shooting day is a social event, and your dog needs to obey even when there are other dogs and people around. He needs to be able to pick out your voice and whistle signals from among others, and he must learn to keep an eye on you and not go off with someone else or their dog. Training classes are an excellent chance to advance your dog's education.

What makes a good instructor? Man or woman, a good instructor is one who can not only train a dog to a high standard, but can also put his views and ideas across to you. He needs to be able to demonstrate his

Training class. The instructor remains close to her dog to give him confidence. (Courtesy Paul Quagliana, Shooting Times)

You must play your part. You should arrive on time, and your dog should have had a chance to empty himself before you come to class. He should not be fed before class. You should park carefully and where you are told. You will need to bring poo bags to clean up after your dog should he make a 'mistake', and be sure to take the bag home with you. If you take dummies to class, make sure your name is on them. Keep your dog on the lead until told you can let him off. Don't let him be a nuisance to other dogs or people. Don't be embarrassed to ask questions, but be considerate to others. Make sure to do your homework.

own dog and show you the finished article. Equally, he needs to know different ways for you to use so you can achieve a similar standard with your dog. If one way does not work for your dog, then the instructor should be able to teach you another method. It is good if he is patient, but better if he is flexible and can adapt to each dog and each situation as it presents itself. You need encouragement but also constructive criticism. The instructor should have access to different kinds of terrain and water.

But however good your instructor may be, he is not a magician. You cannot expect him to wave a magic wand and your dog will be trained. Your instructor is your guide, but *you* must put in the work.

INTRODUCTION TO LIVE GAME

When you feel confident that your dog is truly obedient and focused on you, when he is reliable at sitting and walking at heel, both on and off the lead, and when you know that he is word perfect on the recall, it is time to progress to training him to behave in the presence of live game. Having said that, I feel it is very helpful if you have introduced him to other animals first, such as cattle, sheep, horses and chickens. If he will pay attention to you in the presence of these live creatures, he is more likely to pay attention to you when you take him to a release pen.

Perhaps you have already located a rabbit pen and

started teaching your dog good manners in tempting conditions. If not, you could start with penned chickens in order to make the step up to introducing him to live game easier than taking him straight into a pen full of wild birds. Obviously you need permission from the owner of the chickens, and you must assure him that none of his hens will be chased or harmed by your dog. You must keep your dog on the lead until you are absolutely sure that he will obey you when unleashed. Treat the chickens as you would sheep (*see* Chapter 5): with chickens and sheep, when your dog shows any interest, you should use the word 'Leave', which means 'Never'. With rabbits and gamebirds you should say 'Sit', because you mean 'Not now'.

At no time should you walk straight towards the chickens or rabbits with the dog, as this will be seen by the dog as the two of you 'hunting' or stalking the quarry together.

When you find that you can walk your dog at heel off the lead through a rabbit or chicken pen safely, you are ready to introduce him to gamebirds at close quarters. Make enquiries and find a friendly gamekeeper. Explain that you have a young dog which has reached the stage in his training where he needs to be exposed to live game. Assure the keeper that your dog will not at any time be allowed to chase his birds. If he is willing for you to come, be punctual.

Gamekeepers are extremely busy people, but they are often very helpful, especially when they find a dog handler who wants his dog to be an asset to a shoot, not a liability. Keepers are always on the lookout for dogs which might be useful on their shoot. Offer your help, and he may ask you to 'dog in' for him. This is done when pheasants are recently released and involves beating the bounds to keep them on the shoot, and rounding up the birds in the late afternoon and persuading them to go back to their pen to roost. This is a very responsible job, and one for which your dog needs to be absolutely under control. It is also very time-consuming. Spaniel people will quarter their spaniels to drive the birds home. Your Labrador should walk to heel or can be told to sit as a kind of sentry while you move the birds.

The keeper will probably take you to a pen and tell you where you should and should not go. Be sure to stick to his directions. He may well stay to watch and see how obedient your dog is. Ask to be allowed to stand and walk with your dog both outside and inside the release pen.

Be aware of where birds are, and do not put your dog under too much temptation. You must not let him off the lead unless you are certain you can control him.

Insist that your dog watches the birds calmly. If he is so overwrought that he cannot be calm, you must keep him on the lead. Do your utmost to get him to focus on you, saying 'Sit', and drawing your hand from his nose up to your face. Try using a titbit to make him look up at your face. Start by putting the treat near his nose, and when his attention is on the food, draw it slowly up towards your face so that his eyes follow your hand. If he keeps his gaze fixed on your hand, quickly stoop down and place the treat in his mouth. If he won't look at you, he doesn't receive a reward. Certainly, you must not give him food if he is still staring at the birds or rabbits. If you try this three or four times and he will not focus on you, hurry him off home and put him in his quiet place.

You should practise in places where there are gamebirds as often as you are allowed. Your dog should acknowledge the presence of the birds but should at no time disobey you or move towards them. Eventually you will know that he is obedient enough to do a recall or a simple retrieve near the birds – though proceed with extreme caution. If your dog breaks his steadiness and begins to chase, you will have gone a long way backwards both with his training and in the eyes of the keeper.

INTRODUCTION TO RETRIEVING GAME

Retrieving game is another aspect of training your Labrador which should be introduced gradually. Up to now, you may well have been telling your dog to ignore live game – but now, in his opinion, you are contradicting yourself and asking him to pick it up! Of course, it is not quite like that. What you want him to do is to retrieve dead game, which smells quite different: he must still resist the temptation to chase live, undamaged game.

It is not always easy to acquire dead game just when you want it, but if you ask a gamekeeper or gundog trainer, they may have something you can use. In the shooting season it should be easy for you to obtain birds. I keep a few dead pheasants, grouse, pigeon and partridge in the feather in my freezer all the year round. They do not have to be thawed before you ask your dog to retrieve them. If you come by a dead pigeon, be sure to put it inside a stocking before asking your dog to retrieve it, because pigeon feathers come out very easily and can put off a young dog. A rabbit is usually very attractive to any dog. If the animal has been badly shot, do not use it. The blood or damage may encourage a young dog to lick or chew the carcass.

Show the bird or rabbit to your dog, and let him inspect it thoroughly. Tell him to sit while you walk away, and let him see you place the carcass so it is partially hidden in tufty grass. If you are using a bird, place it so that its back is uppermost – it is easiest for a dog to carry a bird with his mouth over its back. I do not throw the game, partly out of respect but partly so that it is not too exciting. Return to your dog and send it with 'Hie lost' and the chop signal – you have changed the picture enough by walking out and back and so on to make this an unseen retrieve.

A moment after the dog reaches the quarry and dips his head to inspect or pick it, blow your recall whistle and give your voice command to call him back. Hopefully, he will pick up the retrieve and bring it straight back without fuss. If so, make much of him and put him away in his quiet place. Most dogs, however, sniff the carcass and are in two minds about what to do with it. Give him a few seconds, then call him again. This time he must come, whether he brings the retrieve or not.

If he comes back to you without it he will probably be regretting that he did not bring the carcass with him. Give him a few moments to 'think it over', then send him again. Most dogs will bring the retrieve this time but if he still does not, go out with him and make a bit of a game of it. Pick the bird up by a wing, or if a rabbit, by a leg, and pull it around gently in a circle close to the ground to entice the dog. If he makes a grab at it, praise him and see if he will take it from you. There will be plenty of time to resolve any blips in his behaviour

as training goes on, but get him keen on taking hold of game now.

If he starts to be silly or tries to bite or chew the carcass, however, you will have to call a halt. Take the carcass from him and offer it to him dorsal side first. See if he will take it nicely – but you should not let go of it. Praise him and share it with him. After a few seconds say 'Dead', and take it from him. If he is reluctant to give it up, try covering his eyes; this often works because it makes a dog feel disadvantaged, just as the muzzle-holding technique does. If he still will not let go, do not let yourself get cross, but gently prise his jaws apart and take it. Let that do for the day, and put him in his quiet place.

If he refuses absolutely to have anything to do with the carcass, put it away, do something you know he is confident in doing, then put him away in his quiet place. Almost certainly, when you approach this subject a day or two later, he will have thought about it and wished he had done the retrieve. It sounds anthropomorphic to say this, but it often seems to work this way; it has to do with instinct and the memory pathways you have been building in his brain during training. He may well do a perfect retrieve when you approach the matter afresh.

If, however, the young dog persists in avoiding picking game, try to engender some jealousy by letting him watch an older, experienced dog retrieve. Do not let the youngster snatch the retrieve from the other dog, but if he does show interest, let him strain at the lead and nearly take it; then try him again on the retrieve himself. If this does not work, leave the subject for a couple of weeks before you try again.

The dog that will happily pick up and carry cold game will usually transfer quite easily and quickly to warm game, but a halfway house would be to leave a cold bird in a warm place – in an airing cupboard in a plastic bag, say, until the chill is off it. If you have a partner or family, it would be best to discuss your plans with them first – and don't forget where you left the bird! When you want to try the dog on it, take the bird outdoors, show it to him, and then place it as you did the first, cold, bird. All should be well, but make sure to call him up quickly as soon as he picks up the bird.

Until your dog is ready to go out shooting, you cannot introduce him to wounded game. In the United

Kingdom wounded birds are called runners (in North America they are called cripples). Great care must be taken when first trying your young dog on wounded game, because it does cause confusion in his mind. It is akin to the confusion mentioned above where the dog has been admonished for showing an interest in live game, and next you want him to pick up game, albeit dead. Now you are saying that he can pick up live game! Be this as it may, he will soon realize that this live game has a different smell – it has a blood scent, and probably the scent that adrenalin causes. Care must be taken because this new idea can cause great excitement in the dog, which can lead to roughness or biting.

Ideally, the first retrieve of a wounded animal should be on one which is still alive but unable to move. When the dog is confident about retrieving this, try him on a runner – though you must not send him while the animal is still in sight, as this can lead to him chasing any running game. Let the runner make it to cover, then take the dog to the fall and encourage him to 'take a line' (this means he should follow the scent trail until he finds the quarry). It is best if you can keep the dog in view so that as soon as he has the runner in his mouth you can recall him as quickly as possible. He must not have time to think of playing with it or eating it.

Some trainers advocate a system of dragging a carcass on a line to lay a trail for the dog to follow, but I have never done this. My dogs have all learned to take a line naturally and follow scent in the right direction. It is an innate talent that Labradors have, particularly if they are from good working lines.

INTRODUCTION TO GUNFIRE

You began to accustom your young dog to loud noises when he was quite a puppy by slamming a book shut and bursting a paper bag in another room before feeding time. Gradually you moved closer, as long as he appeared to tolerate the noise. At training classes, your youngster will probably have heard the report of a starting pistol or dummy launcher.

However, if you have not gone to classes, you will need to ask a friend to help you. Preferably he should use a .410-gauge shotgun for the first gun-training

session. Put some biscuits in your pocket, and move yourself and your dog about a hundred paces away from your helper. Take a biscuit in your hand, and signal for the gun to be fired into the air. The moment you hear the report, give the dog the biscuit. If your dog appears anxious at the sound of the report but will eat the biscuit, give him another, but move further away from the gun before repeating the exercise. Let that do for that day, and put the dog in his quiet place. As time goes by, you will find that you can move closer to the gun or let the gun come closer to you.

If your dog is not afraid of the .410, move a bit closer and ask your helper to fire a second shot and throw a dummy out to his side. Send your dog to retrieve. Let that do, put the lead on and take him to his quiet place. On a subsequent day, ask your assistant to fire a 12 bore at approximately fifty paces. Give the dog a treat, and if he has shown no fear, ask for another shot with a throw. After your dog has retrieved the dummy, put him away as before.

When it comes to a shoot day, you must not take your new entry into line with you. You should position yourself and your dog out of range of the Guns or behind trees or some other barrier. Have some cotton wool in your pocket in case the dog shows anxiety: you can put it in his ears to deaden the sharpness of the bangs – though remember to take it out after the drive so he can hear you and your whistle when you are sending him to retrieve! If he seems unconcerned by the shooting you can move closer for the next drive, perhaps positioning yourself behind the Guns' vehicles for protection. As with every other aspect of training, handle this one step by step, remembering that you can only build on success.

Most Labradors from good working lines look interested rather than frightened when they first hear a gun fired, but a significant number show anxiety or fear. This is gun nervousness, not gunshyness. With sympathetic management, a dog will lose his nervousness and become very keen as soon as he makes the connection between the bang and the retrieve.

A dog that is truly gunshy will show real terror, and if off lead will run home or go under a car or find some other hiding place, and will be very difficult to coax out. A friend's Viszla ran and kept running and was found some distance away in the next county the following day. Strangely, this was a dog which was very keen and excited at the report of a dummy launcher, but she could not tolerate a shotgun.

Many people believe gunshyness is incurable, but I have heard of a few successes. In one case I had a Labrador to train called Mamba, who was so frightened of bangs she would run back to the kennel if she saw me with the game bag over my shoulder. She could not be still in a vehicle if it was anywhere near shooting, but would dash around inside the car and rip up the interior. Very disappointed, the owner decided to acquire another trained dog, Bracken, but kept Mamba as a pet. As time went on and Bracken came home smelling of game and fun, Mamba gradually became extremely interested in her. After a while she would come happily to shoots in the car and wait eagerly for Bracken's return, making a huge fuss of her and sniffing her all over. To make a long story short, Mamba eventually came out shooting and enjoyed it as much as any good gundog. She also became an efficient game-finder.

CHAPTER 11

'THE REAL THING'

The shooting season is in the offing, and you are wondering if your Labrador is ready for 'the real thing'. To help you make up your mind, you need to ask yourself the following questions and answer them honestly. Does he come to you reliably under all conditions? Will he stop on the whistle at a fair distance in the face of temptation? Does he walk nicely to heel on and off lead without repeated reminders? If the answer to any of these questions is 'No', then you must accept that he is just not ready yet.

I am very definite on this subject because I have learnt that if you take a dog into 'battle conditions' before he has reached an advanced stage in his training, he will never forget the feelings he experienced on that first outing. No matter how much training you give him after that, he will always remember that day for the state of high excitement that built up both inside him and around him, the pure joy of losing his head – even if kept on the lead – or, worst case scenario, running wild and ignoring his handler. Remembering how memory pathways are formed in the brain (see Chapter 4, The Physiology of Learning), it seems that sometimes it takes only one thoroughly enjoyable experience to make a memory everlasting! However, if your dog has a good grounding in obedience and is focused on you, he will be excited, but he will have that degree of self-discipline which inhibits him when instinct is aroused. If you think you can rely on his obedience, then proceed.

The early shooting days must be tackled in different ways according to whether you are going to shoot, or to pick up. Picking-up is a very satisfying and rewarding pastime, and shooting over your own dog can make you very proud. Many situations and etiquettes apply in both shooting over your dog and picking-up with him, so I urge you to read both sections.

SHOOTING OVER YOUR LABRADOR

When you receive your invitation, ask your host if it is all right for you to bring your dog, and if you will go in shoot transport or in your own vehicle. If the latter, you need to enquire if four-wheel drive is needed; if the former, you will have to be very organized and have everything you need with you for both yourself and your dog. Put your dog on the lead when you take him out of your car, and keep him on the lead in the shoot wagon.

Before taking your dog out shooting, make a list of the things you should have with you. In addition to the things you need for yourself, you will need the following for the dog: lead, whistle, towel or a towelling coat, first-aid kit, food if you are staying late or overnight, water and bowls. You should also have a priest for dispatching wounded birds.

The first time you take your dog on a shoot, a counsel of perfection would be that you do not shoot. Your whole attention should be on your dog. In fact, your dog should not come into the shooting line. Although he may be perfectly happy with one or two shots, you do not know how he will react to a barrage. In the previous chapter, we discussed how the introduction to gunfire should be made.

Walked-up shooting and rough shooting are good ways of getting a dog used to gunfire because the shooting is sporadic, and the result, if you are lucky, is a retrieve. This will cheer up a dog that is anxious about the report of a gun. However, he soon learns when his handler is not paying full attention to him, so you must be careful that you have your mind on the dog first, and

The finished article – the handler is able to concentrate on his shooting knowing his dog is steady and obedient.

the shooting second. A good policy is to make a habit of saying 'Sit' as you take off the safety catch – eventually it will be second nature for the dog to sit when he hears the click of the catch.

In due course your dog will be happy to be in line with you. But now, especially, you must keep both mind and eye on your dog, because if he runs-in even just once, you may never be able to reinstate steadiness. In my mind's eye I can see Tom, a shooting friend, who had a young dog with him at one of the shoots where I pick up. He had trained the dog himself, and this was her third or fourth outing. But in the middle of a drive, she took off after a shot bird. Tom unloaded his gun, laid it on the ground, and took off after the dog and actually caught up with her before she reached the bird. He scolded her all the way back to her proper place, then sat her down with a 'Good dog' where she remained. I

admired him very much for that, and the dog believed from then on that Tom was always paying attention, which he mostly was. He may have missed a bit of the shooting, but the benefit to his dog in the long term was huge.

Do not allow your dog to retrieve during a drive as it is distracting to everyone, especially you. It can also lead to your dog getting out of hand, perhaps going into a covert which is to be the next drive. If there is a runner, let the pickers-up see to it.

If your neighbouring Gun has a dog, ask him before the drive if he will want his dog to retrieve all his own birds; also, do not retrieve another Gun's birds if he has his own dog unless you have spoken about it with him. It is possible that he does not want his dog to retrieve runners. Really, you should not ask your dog to pick anything that you could pick yourself. Easy birds will make him gleeful and he may start playing with them, tossing them or, worst of all, eating them.

Whatever your dog retrieves, make sure, if it is a runner, that it is quickly and humanely dispatched with a priest or the pliers-type of dispatcher. Leave the birds neatly spaced out near your peg, and not in a heap, because they need to cool. Tell whoever is in charge exactly where you have left them, and how many there are. Often time is too short for Guns to pick-up thoroughly after a drive, so if you know you have left some or you have seen a bird go a long way, try to get a message to the pickers-up.

Walked-up shooting is the very best way of achieving good heelwork under temptation, especially if you are not carrying a gun and can give your whole attention to the dog. Shooting over pointers or setters is very exciting for retrievers: they soon learn to watch the dogs

questing in front, and become electrified at the sight of a point because they know that this presages shooting and, with luck, a retrieve.

PICKING-UP WITH YOUR LABRADOR

First and foremost, a picker-up should remember that a shoot day is the Guns' day. They pay for the day, and without them, none of us would be there. Obviously this is on commercial days, but even if the Guns are guests, it is still their day. Pickers-up, even if paid, are there as a privilege, and they must make sure that they do not spoil the day for the Guns.

Probably the best day to bring out your newly trained Labrador would be a small day, one of eighty to a hundred birds. Ideally there should be a general appreciation of well behaved dogs – although we do

The 'dogmobile' full of picking-up dogs.

not live in an ideal world! However, even on a day when all the other dogs run wild, your dog can come home having learnt something good. Do not compete with other handlers' dogs for retrieves, but keep your dog steady, and when things go quiet, take a dead bird and set up a retrieve for him in a secluded corner and make him do it correctly. Many people believe their dog becomes frustrated and disappointed when they do not have anything to retrieve. Perhaps they do, but life isn't fair, and dogs need to accept the situation just as we do. For dogs, a shoot day involves a lot of waiting, and it requires a lot of patience and discipline. So do not become irritable because the dog will sense it, and may follow suit. Let him see that you are calm, and he will relax and also accept the situation.

Preparation and Protocol

On receiving your invitation, you should find out the following: where to meet and what time, where to park, what time the Guns move off. Ask who you should report to when you arrive. Should you bring lunch? Do you walk everywhere, or should you take your own vehicle, or is one provided? Do you need four-wheel drive? Are you paid, or are you given a brace of birds and/or lunch instead? Do not expect to be paid if you are a beginner or if you have a single beginner dog.

Make a list of the things you will need and keep the list at hand so that you can refer to it each time you go picking up. My list consists of boots or Wellies, the right socks, waterproof leggings, coat, hat, scarf, gloves, ear defenders, change of shoes if you go in for lunch, picnic lunch if you don't, dogs, whistles, leads, water and bowl, priest and/or stick (your third leg), game carrier, dogs' coats, money for sweepstake, paper and pencil for notes, and a first aid kit. In addition I carry arnica pills (for the dogs and for me), a penknife, wire cutters, a belt to use as an extra lead if necessary, lipsalve,

Dogs can be safely left in their car cage at the shoot meet and between drives.

hankies, paracetamol and sweets. I have a dry coat or jacket in the car for myself in case it is a very wet day, then I can drive home in relative comfort.

Arrive at the meet in good time, having ensured that your dog or dogs have had a chance to empty themselves before leaving home. Keep them in the car until you are ready to move off, or until you come to the first drive.

When you first take your dog out of the car, have him on the lead. Even the most experienced handler's dog may chase a stray bird, deer or hare, or the host's chickens, or get into a scrap with someone else's dog. You only need to take your mind off a dog for a moment and he will get into mischief.

Report to your contact – the host, gamekeeper or chief picker-up – for your instructions. Obtain a list of the drives if there is one. On some shoots you will be given a radio so that you can communicate with the other pickers-up. Sometimes you will be on the same frequency as the shoot captain and the keeper, and you should find out if this is so. Whatever the case, speak only if spoken to or if you are in doubt or difficulty. Be a listener rather than a talker.

If you are being provided with a vehicle, find out which one it is and who will drive. If you are to travel with others, make sure you have everything you will need with you. It is better to have too much clothing than not enough; you can always shed some of your layers, but it is awful to be too cold or to get soaked to the skin for no good reason.

Always go back to the vehicle you were assigned to after a drive, or, if your plan changes, leave a note on it for your fellow pickers-up to say what you are doing, otherwise they may wait for you and miss the next drive! It is always a wise precaution to know where the next drive is in case you should be left behind. When should you stop picking-up and go back to the vehicle? You will only learn that through instinct and experience!

When you think you have cleared your area, take your birds to the game cart or do what you have been instructed. If the birds have been laid out on the ground and your dog shows an interest or tries to help himself, he should be scolded. He can tell when a bird has already been in a human hand or a dog's mouth. Sometimes, in training or competition, you may ask

him to retrieve such a bird, but when there are several in a group or (heaven forbid) a pile, he should leave them alone.

Never, ever leave game in a vehicle where it can be got at by a dog. To a dog it is food and you cannot be surprised, let alone cross, if your dog makes a meal of it. The dog can be the best trained, most gentlemanly, most well fed animal in the world, but if you leave him with food, he may eat it. And once he has had the opportunity to eat game, he will think it is permitted and will do it again if he can.

Pickers-up should not drive in front of the Guns, but should park their vehicles behind the Guns' vehicles or somewhere that the keeper approves. Do not make unnecessary noise when getting out, and do not open the back of the vehicle until all handlers are ready for their dogs.

Ask your fellow pickers-up if you should pick-up during the drive or wait until the end. Usually only runners should be collected during the drive, but if your dog is very green, you should not let him do this. Talk to the others and ask them to cover for you. Perhaps one will even stand with you.

Ascertain where your fellow pickers-up will be, where you should stand and where your 'patch' is (during and after the drive), and where to meet up after that drive. Ensure that you are not in a position where you could be shot. If you are told to be uphill behind the Guns, you must find a barrier to shield you, otherwise refuse to stand there. This is not just because it is unsafe for you, but it is very off-putting to a Gun to turn and see you there. It just should not happen. If you are in any doubt at all, speak to the Guns in front and ask tactfully if you are in their way. This tells them where you will be. Once they know that you are there, do not move substantially during the drive.

Make sure you are not a blot on the landscape or standing out on the skyline. You may possibly turn birds or make a keeper nervous that you will turn them.

Be certain where subsequent drives are so you don't let your dog into a covert that will be beaten later. If in any doubt at all, ask exactly where you can and cannot pick up for that drive. Also check where the nearest release pens are, and whether the keeper wants them avoided. It is very easy to 'peg' birds in and around the release pens, and there are always untouched birds there, and huge numbers of them at the beginning of the season. Once you and your dog have proved your reliability you may be granted the honour of being allowed to pick-up in the pens, but it is a great privilege given only to trusted pickers-up with very polite, controllable dogs.

Protocol with the Guns

Before a drive begins you should go up to the Guns who are nearest you and who have a dog or dogs and ask if they want to pick all their birds, or if they would like you to pick runners behind them during the drive. Pickers-up should not send their dogs for birds in front of the Guns during a drive. If a Gun wishes to use his dog after the drive, keep an eye on him to make sure he has collected all the birds in his area. A Gun cannot be absolutely sure how many birds he has had down, or where they are exactly, because he will have been concentrating on his shooting. A picker-up is primarily there for the difficult, distant and wounded birds – not the easy ones close to the Guns. Ideally you should be well back from the Guns, but there are exceptions to this because you need to see where birds are falling.

Be aware that some shoots may not like you to speak to the Guns at all, indeed, you may be out of sight of them all day. The keeper or the pickers-up captain will tell you what the form is. If you are standing in line beside a Gun, only speak if spoken to once the drive starts, as you should not distract the Gun's attention from his shooting.

On partridge days you will often be asked to stand in line with the Guns. Turn off your mobile phone, and stand absolutely in line equidistant between two Guns: this will be your safest place as Guns should never shoot down the line – that is, at each other – so you should be all right.

A Gun should make sure that there is lots of lovely sky around every bird he shoots at. Usually ground game is forbidden on driven days. If a Gun shoots low and you find yourself looking down his barrels, you must tell the shoot captain or the keeper as soon as possible, because next time someone might be killed. It is an unenviable task to report unsafe shooting because you might be criticizing one of the host's closest friends. It may be helpful if you can find someone else who witnessed the event and who is willing to back you up. And if your words are not taken well, ask yourself if you really wish to continue on a shoot which condones dangerous shooting.

Some Other Dos and Don'ts

Always bear in mind that the quick dispatch of wounded game is essential if shooting is to keep a good profile in the eyes of the general public. We must give the 'antis' as little reason to attack us as we can. Ask someone who is experienced to show you how to dispatch game humanely.

Do not send your dog for a bird when another dog is already questing for it. First of all it is impolite, and secondly, it will probably muddle the scent for both dogs.

Be as quiet as you can when handling your dog. Don't shout at him, however cross you are, and use a minimum of whistling or arm waving if you are in sight of the Guns. Don't shout at, or for, your fellow pickers-up! In fact, don't shout!

If you are picking-up near a road, remember that it is never worth having your valuable and beloved Labrador run over for the sake of a pheasant. Stand with your back to the road and work away from it in the hope that you will also push away any runners – but be aware that they may turn and pass you, followed by your dog! Personally I will not work my dog near a road. I will try to pick birds with my dog on the lead, but if that is not possible, I tell the keeper of any that I have seen land near or across the road.

There should be a whistle or horn blown to signal the end of each drive. If you are out of sight of the Guns but think the drive is over, go forwards very carefully in case it is just a lull, and see if guns are being put in their slips. If you are sure the drive has ended, go up to the Guns to see what is still left to be collected. They may have seen birds down that you missed. Check around the pegs and pick up any birds left by the Guns, and take them back to the game cart with the others you have retrieved.

Looking After your Dog

The beauty of having a trained dog, one of the many beauties, is that he saves his energy by going when and where he is told, and returning immediately on the recall whistle. And you will find that you are not so tired at the end of the day as you would be with the sort of dog which yanks and lunges at the end of the lead, which charges about aimlessly, swaps birds, and will not come when called. This sort of dog also has to be put on the lead again as he gives you his latest retrieve – you almost need two pairs of hands!

A shoot day is very testing for a dog. In the first place, he is not used to staying awake for more than a couple of hours at a time. A dog normally sleeps for most of the day, and it is important that we keep this in mind because a tired dog can become forgetful, and after a certain length of time his training may not stick in his mind very well. He may make mistakes, and you may become cross, which would not be a good thing. As a rule, I only have a young dog out for two drives at a time. This means that you must have somewhere to put him while you continue, and it must be ventilated, secure and unchewable. Usually this would be a cage in a car with its windows open and perhaps the tailgate kept open with a special device such as a Ventlock. A dog left behind may become very agitated and attack his surroundings: the interior of many a vehicle has been destroyed by a dog's teeth.

At lunchtime and at the end of the day, give your dog a quick check for ticks, thorns and cuts. Make sure he is warm and comfortable and has fresh water available.

Another bird for the bag.

Working More than one Dog at a Time

If you become a keen picker-up, you will soon find that you need more than one dog. With only one dog, it is a certainty that while he is out hunting for one bird, another injured one will fall which needs speedy collection.

When I started, a friend said, 'You always ruin your first dog.' This is not a kind thing to say, but it is quite close to the truth, as I have discovered. 'Ruin' is perhaps a bit too strong, but without doubt, the first dog is a case of feeling your way and a steep learning curve. Every dog is different and will present you with new puzzles and challenges, but your abilities will improve and each dog should be better than, if different from, the last.

When you acquire your second dog, and any subsequent ones, an essential matter to consider is name. Make sure that each name is different from any of the others, and not like the names of dogs belonging to people with whom you train frequently.

You will need to be self-disciplined and take out each dog separately until their steadiness is good. When you begin to train the two together, you must teach yourself to keep your eye on the youngster most of the time, especially when you send the older dog to retrieve, so that you maintain the younger dog's steadiness. Always preface your commands with the relevant dog's name.

The Joys of Picking Up

Every shoot is different, and that is part of the attraction of picking-up: you will see new parts of the country, new terrain, different people, the individual ways of running a day – all are so interesting. Nevertheless picking-up is a solitary pastime and not for someone who does not like his own company; but if you are happy on your own and do not mind bad weather, you will see birds and animals that otherwise you might not. You will sometimes find mushrooms, fruits and nuts to take home – though make sure with your host that this is all right.

Be sure to thank your host and/or the keeper at the end of the day, and let the latter know of any birds you were unable to collect.

Above all, the enjoyment derived from picking up with dogs you have trained yourself is immense.

The picking-up team.

CHAPTER 12

COMPETITION

There are two main types of gundog competition: working tests and field trials. The subject of competition warrants a book of its own, but in essence, competition gives you a chance to compare your dog's standard with that of other dogs, and your training and handling ability with that of other handlers.

WORKING TESTS

Most gundog clubs hold working tests. Most are held under Kennel Club rules and guidelines, and these require first and foremost that all dogs entered are registered with the Kennel Club. Competitors must abide by Kennel Club regulations, and a booklet of the rules and guidelines can be obtained by contacting The Kennel Club. Some competitions are held in aid of charities, which may or may not be affiliated to The Kennel Club. Unregistered dogs may compete in these. Usually the organizers will wish to adhere to Kennel Club guidelines with regard to safety, placing dummies, firing shots, judging, scoring and certain other aspects.

Before you enter a competition you should know what is expected of you. Bitches in season must not be brought to the ground. You should dress tidily in neutral colours – there is no specific uniform, but sombre browns and greens are much in evidence. Except in the designated exercise areas, your dog should be kept on the lead until you go into line.

Pay close attention when the judge is explaining a test to you. Pass the dummy to your judge as soon as you have taken it from the dog, and never throw it on the ground: if it were a bird you would not throw it down.

You should not touch your dog except in praise when an exercise is completed.

Once you take the lead off, you must put it away in your pocket – you are not allowed to carry anything in your hand, although if you need a walking stick, you should ask the judge's permission to have it with you.

During competition, you should be as quiet in handling your dog as possible. Extra commands and noisy handling will be penalized, and verbal or physical correction is not permitted.

Working tests are held mainly in the summer months, and are a good day out, especially if the weather is kind. They give you the opportunity to discuss training matters with people who share the same interest as you, and, as with training classes, you have someone else to organize your day and put you and your dog through your paces. It is a good idea to go as a spectator a few times to see what sort of thing is required so that you can prepare for your dog's debut.

When you enter a competition, make sure you leave home in plenty of time so that you do not arrive at the ground feeling rushed and irritable. Allow time for exercising your dog when you reach the ground, and for him to empty himself. Clean up after him and take the poo bags home.

If in a test you are faced with a situation which is too much for your dog, ask the judge if you may go forward and help him so that he learns something good. It is better to sacrifice points when you are struggling than to let your dog learn something bad and still lose points.

FIELD TRIALS

Field trials give you the opportunity to show your dog's working abilities at the highest level. Nowadays trials are run exclusively under Kennel Club rules. Retriever

Field triallers enjoying a fine September day.

field trials are meant to be run as closely as possible to an ordinary day's shooting, and are held during the game-shooting season, which runs from August to February. You can find out which clubs hold trials in your area by contacting The Kennel Club. Get in touch with a few field trial club secretaries and ask if you may come and help or spectate at their trials before entering one. You must know what is expected of you and your dog beforehand.

Before you apply to enter a trial you must be sure that your dog has had sufficient experience in the shoot-

ing field. He must be confident on runners. He should have picked a variety of game as he may be required to retrieve anything from a tiny snipe to a ten-pound goose. He must be absolutely steady under temptation, he must not make any noise whatever in a shooting situation, he must be obedient and under control, and he must have a soft mouth.

Whether it is a test or a trial, remember these things. A training fault in your dog is probably your fault. The dog you arrived with in the morning is the same dog you are taking home with you, and he doesn't mind if he has won or not. You thought he was good enough to enter him in competition, but if you find that he isn't, it's up to you to bring him up to standard.

From time to time you come across a dog which is superb in every way as a gamefinder, a dog with style, stamina and a good mouth, which jumps and swims willingly and gets game in the bag. But sadly, this dog is not quite what is wanted for competition because he has an eliminating fault. It could be that he is unsteady or a little bit noisy. This is what you might call your 'rough-and-ready' dog. If you are not interested in competition, it is not altogether a bad thing to have a dog of this sort – a dog which runs-in or makes a tiny noise during a drive can be a real asset. You don't have to be on the alert the entire time in order to keep this sort of dog up to competition standard. You can have him on a lead and let him go for runners 'on the bounce' without worrying that this will make him unsteady – he already is. This sort of dog is extremely useful in a picking-up situation because it means that you can keep your competition dog 'on ice' and only send him when you want to and when you can give him your full attention. The 'rough-and-ready' dog can do the rest.

Some competition-minded people do not take their

Walked-up partridge shooting for a Labrador field trial.

field trial dogs picking-up at all, and I find this astonishing. I feel that picking up teaches a dog gun sense and game sense. He learns how a gamebird thinks and where it is likely to go, he learns to persevere when scent is poor, and he learns to negotiate obstacles when he is out of sight of his handler.

To win a field trial carries much prestige and increases a dog's value both intrinsically and from a breeding point of view. It also gives you a buzz which few other things can equal!

'A judgely huddle' – three field trial judges conferring.

TAILPIECE

I began this book in 1979, and wrote it by hand. Just as I finished it, my life became extremely busy and the book was shelved. About ten years went by. Then one day I took out the manuscript and began to type it out neatly. As I progressed, I was shocked. 'Did I really think that? Is this the way I taught that?' I had learned different, fairer ways, and had discarded slow and confusing methods. I shelved the manuscript again.

A lot of water has gone under the bridge since then, and a great many things in the gundog world have changed. Certainly the competitions and the ways of

Is that bird coming my way?

judging and handling have changed, and the dogs have changed: they are more biddable, but are still bold and athletic. When I first ran in trials three or four dogs might be lost, sometimes more, in the first drive through unsteadiness. Whining and hard mouth, I seem to remember, were much more prevalent. Nowadays, however, running-in seldom occurs in trials, whining is far less common than it used to be, and hard mouth is rarely encountered. Obedience to the whistle and hand signals has improved greatly.

The fine tuning you see in tests and trials nowadays is remarkable. Tests have been devised that provide extreme challenges to dog and handler. Much emphasis is placed on how well the dog responds to his handler. The standard is so high it sometimes seems like splitting hairs to decide between the dogs. There are those who say that trialling has become a sport in its own right, and I am inclined to agree. However, I hope and believe that there are dogs which can wait patiently and quietly in line and make their owner proud, which can do a good day's picking-up on one day, and run well in a trial the following day. That's my sort of dog.

I like a gundog to show style, game-finding ability, initiative and perseverance, but also control. I like a dog that will handle to the area where I believe the retrieve to be, and then hunt. I do not want him to think I will tell him which blade of grass to look behind: he should get on with the job himself and not repeatedly turn to me for help.

We are an amazing species for passing on ideas and information. Life really is a learning process. I may well change my ideas on gundog training again and again as time goes on, but just now I would like to pass on what I have found to work well in producing a good all-round working Labrador for use in the shooting field. I believe my methods will work for you, too.

GLOSSARY

covert (noun) (pronounced 'cover') Woodland in which game is found.

dewclaws (noun) The vestigial toes that some dogs have on the inner 'wrist' or 'ankle' of their front and hind legs. These do not usually touch the ground but those on the forelegs may help dogs clamber over stone walls.

drive (noun) Designated section of land, covert or game crop, with Gun placings beyond, from which beaters drive game. There is usually an average of five drives on an organized shoot day.

drive (verb) To encourage game forwards towards the Guns.

fall (noun) Place where dummy or bird first lands.

flush (noun, verb) When game is caused to rise from its hiding place.

hard mouth (noun) When a dog crushes in the ribs of a bird on one or both sides, or significantly tears or damages game.

line (noun) Scent trail left by running game.

mark (verb) Take note of the fall.

meet (noun) Place where members of the shoot assemble at the start of the day.

prick (verb) To wound (game) slightly.

priest (noun) Weighted stick used to dispatch wounded game by giving it a smart blow on the head.

rough shooting (noun) Usually one or two people with dogs, often spaniels, walking-up hedgerows and over rough game-holding terrain, shooting 'for the pot'.

runner (noun) Wounded gamebird, not necessarily able to run. (American: cripple)

scruff (noun) The loose skin at the back of a dog's neck.

season (noun) The period, usually occurring six monthly and lasting for three weeks, when a bitch is interesting to dogs and during which she can be mated.

shooting season (noun) The periods in the year, which vary according to species, when it is legal to shoot game.

slip (noun) Gun-shaped case used for carrying a shotgun.

style (noun) The way in which a dog works. When a dog looks purposeful in his work and is a pleasure to watch, that would be what I call style.

walked-up shooting (noun) When a shooting party spreads out and walks in line abreast over game-holding ground, often with spaniels or pointers working in front.

wind (verb) To catch scent of game, etc.

12-bore (noun) Shortened term for 12-bore gauge shotgun (similarly, 20-bore).

.410 (noun) Shortened term for a .410-gauge shotgun, sometimes called a poacher's gun.

INDEX

RELATED TITLES FROM CROWOOD

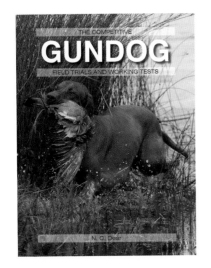

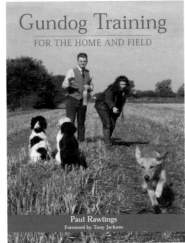

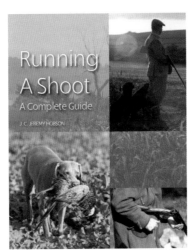

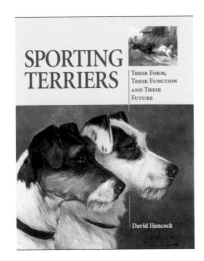